BORGES AT EIGHTY

BORGES
AT EIGHTY

Conversations

Edited and with Photographs by

WILLIS BARNSTONE

INDIANA UNIVERSITY PRESS

Bloomington

Library of Congress Cataloging in Publication Data

Borges, Jorge Luis, 1899–
  Borges at eighty.

  1. Borges, Jorge Luis, 1899–   —Interviews.
  2. Authors, Argentine—20th Century—Interviews.
  I. Barnstone, Willis, 1927–   . II. Title.
  PQ7797.B635Z462   868 [B]   81-47294
  ISBN 0-253-16626-8   AACR2

to William Cagle

Contents

WORKS BY BORGES

Fervor de Buenos Aires, 1923
Inquisiciones, 1925
Luna de enfrente, 1925
Cuadernos de San Martín, 1929
Evariesto Carriego, 1930
Discusión, 1932
Historia universal de la infamia,
  1935
Historia de la eternidad, 1936
Ficciones, 1944
El aleph, 1949
Otras inquisiciones, 1952
El hacedor, 1960
El otro, el mismo, 1964
Para las seis cuerdas, 1965
Elogio de la sombra, 1969
El informe de Brodie, 1970
El oro de los tigres, 1972
Obras completas, 1974
La rosa profunda, 1975
Libro de arena, 1975

La moneda de hierro, 1976
Historia de la noche, 1977

IN ENGLISH TRANSLATION
Ficciones, 1962
Labyrinths, 1964
Dreamtigers, 1964
Other Inquisitions, 1937–1952,
  1964
A Personal Anthology, 1967
Selected Poems, 1923–1967, 1968
The Book of Imaginary Beings,
  1969
The Aleph and Other Stories,
  1933–1969, 1970
Doctor Brodie's Report, 1971
A Universal History of Infamy,
  1972
In Praise of Darkness, 1974
The Book of Sand, 1977
The Gold of the Tigers, 1977

ACKNOWLEDGMENTS

The conversations presented here as numbers 1, 10, and 11, and the readings and commentary included as number 4 constituted the William T. Patten Foundation Lectures for Spring 1980. In 1931 Mr. William T. Patten of Indianapolis made a gift to Indiana University for the establishment of the Patten Foundation. Under the terms of the bequest, there is chosen each year a Patten Professor, who is in residence for one semester or a part of a semester. Additional funds are used to invite Patten Lecturers, who are on campus for a shorter period of time and who are asked to deliver one or two public lectures. Jorge Luis Borges was the Patten Professor for Spring 1980.

The conversation presented as number 2 in this book first appeared as "Thirteen Questions: A Dialogue with Jorge Luis Borges" in *Chicago Review* 31, no. 3, copyright © 1980 by *Chicago Review* and is reprinted with minor revisions by permission of *Chicago Review*.

Portions of "The Dick Cavett Show," May 5, 1980, are reproduced as conversation number 3 by permission of Daphne Productions.

I am grateful to EMECE Editores, S.A., for permission to reprint the Spanish texts of Borges' "G. L. Bürger," "La luna," "Endimión en Latmos," "Las causas," "Un libro," "Mi vida entera," "El mar," "Fragmento," and "Poema conjetural."

For permission to reprint translated works by Borges, I am indebted to the following: Bantam Books, Inc., for "Remorse" and "Camden 1982," tr. Willis Barnstone, from *Modern European Poetry,* ed. Willis Barnstone, copyright © 1966, 1977 by Bantam Books, Inc.; *Chicago Review* for "The Other Tiger," tr. Willis Barnstone, from *Chicago Review* 27, no. 4, copyright © 1976 by *Chicago Review;* Delacorte Press/Seymour Lawrence for "Fragment," tr. Norman Thomas di Giovanni, and "The Sea," tr. John Updike, from *Jorge Luis Borges: Selected Poems 1923–1967,* ed., with an intro. and notes, Norman Thomas di Giovanni, copyright © 1968, 1969, 1970, 1971, 1972 by Jorge Luis Borges, EMECE Editores, S.A., and Norman Thomas di Giovanni; Grove Press, Inc., and Jonathan Cape Ltd for "A Yellow Rose," tr. Anthony Kerrigan, from Jorge Luis Borges, *A Personal Anthology,* ed. Anthony Kerrigan, copyright © 1967 by Grove Press, Inc., with rights held in British Commonwealth except Canada by Jonathan Cape Ltd; Anthony Kerrigan for "Conjectural Poem" and "My Entire Life," tr. Anthony Kerrigan, from *Poems: Jorge Luis Borges* (Dublin: New Writers' Press, 1969), copyright © 1969 by Anthony

Kerrigan; New Directions Publishing Corp. and Penguin Books Ltd for "Borges and I," tr. James E. Irby, from Jorge Luis Borges, *Labyrinths: Selected Stories and Other Writings,* ed. Donald A. Yates and James E. Irby, copyright © 1962, 1964 by New Directions Publishing Corp., with rights held in British Commonwealth except Canada by Penguin Books Ltd.

FOREWORD

On Christmas night in 1975 in Buenos Aires, in an atmosphere of civil tension, Borges and I shared a Christmas dinner. Borges was very grave. We ate the good food, drank good wine and talked, but the underlying national gloom was in our minds. Finally, it was time to go. Since there was a bus and taxi strike, we had to walk, and, being a gentleman, Borges insisted on first accompanying his companion María Kodama home, although she lived at the far end of the large city. But this was not a burden to the blind seventy-five year old poet, for he loved to walk, especially at night, and it gave him an excuse for conversation. In that windy, alert half-light, we slowly crossed the city. As the hours passed Borges seemed to be more and more awake to every oddity in the streets, to the architecture which his blind eyes somehow knew, to the few passersby. Suddenly a bus appeared and María hopped on it, and we headed back to Borges' flat.

Now that María was, we hoped, safely on her way home, there was no way of hurrying Borges. At first I thought he might not know his way, for he stopped every few steps when he made some important point and circled about as if we were lost. But no, he wanted to talk about his sister Nora and their childhood, about the black man he saw shot on the Brazil-Uruguay border some forty years earlier, and about his military ancestors who fought in the civil wars of the nineteenth century. Often his cane would hit against a hole or small ditch in the broken pavement, and each small event offered him the chance to pause, to stretch his cane and to extend his arms and legs in the posture of an actor. As always, I felt that Borges' character and personal talk were at least as profound and witty as his writing and because of this confirmed—at least for me—the writing itself. By dawn we reached his building. Another long night of conversation was over.

The following afternoon we went together to the Saint James Café and for three hours spoke of nothing but Dante and Milton. By the time evening came, I began to feel a curious melancholy. We were now leaving his apartment to go to the restaurant Maxine's for supper. I said to him: "Borges, I will always remember vaguely your words, my animation, but really none of the words." Borges took me by the arm and, in typical paradoxical consolation, said: "Remember what Swedenborg wrote, that God gave us a brain so that we would have the capacity to forget."

It is impossible for me to remember the words of so many hours on planes, in cars, in streets, in restaurants, and in living rooms, but, at least in this slightly more formal way, his amazing candor, bewilderment, and intelligence are recorded for us all. In my experience nobody's conversation has held such Socratic qualities, the profound and amusing meditation and retort. How lucky we are to have a record of his thought, of a few hours of the conversations which he has shared with others throughout his life in his much esteemed art of friendship.

For three days in 1976 Jorge Luis Borges was at Indiana University in order to participate in a series of public conversations on his life and writings. For a month in the spring of 1980 he returned to Indiana University as a Patten Professor under the joint auspices of the William T. Patten Foundation, the Department of Spanish and Portuguese, the Department of Comparative Literature, and the Office of Latino Affairs. As director of Latino Affairs, Jorge Oclander served as co-host for Borges' visit to the Indiana University campus and, as an Argentine himself, evokes the special character of Buenos Aires, Borges' home, in the Afterword to this volume.

Also during his 1980 visit, Borges traveled to Chicago, New York, and Boston for other talks. He spoke to a large group at the University of Chicago. At the New York PEN Club he was interviewed by Alastair Reid and John Coleman. He appeared on the Dick Cavett show. In the Butler Library at Columbia University he addressed a vast, alert audience. There he said: "A crowd is an illusion. No such thing exists. I am talking to you personally." From New York Borges went to the Massachusetts Institute of Technology, where he participated in a discussion sponsored by Boston University, Harvard University, and MIT. This was Borges' first visit to Cambridge since 1967, when he had been the Charles Eliot Norton Professor of Poetry at Harvard.

The photographs of Borges included in this volume were taken in Buenos Aires, 1976–77.

WILLIS BARNSTONE

BORGES AT EIGHTY

1

The Secret Islands

Indiana University,
March 1980

Why not speak of another secret island? Why not speak of Manhattan? When one thinks of Manhattan, one thinks of New York as being a public city. Yet you are blinded by it as you are blinded by the sun. The sun of course is secret. Only eagles, we are told, are allowed to look at the sun. And I cannot look on New York, not because I am blind, but because I am blinded by it. At the same time I love it. When I speak of New York, I think instantly of Walt Whitman.

JORGE OCLANDER: Everyone sitting in this audience wants to know Jorge Luis Borges.

JORGE LUIS BORGES: I wish I did. I am sick and tired of him.

OCLANDER: Would you take us on a voyage through your own library? Which books did you enjoy reading when you were a young man?

BORGES: Those books are the books I enjoy now. I began reading Stevenson, reading Kipling, reading the Bible, reading the *Arabian Nights* in the Edward William Lane translation, and later the Burton version, and I am still rereading those books. I have done but little reading in my life and much rereading. My eyesight left me for reading purposes, left me in 1955, and since then I have attempted no contemporary reading. I don't think I have read a newspaper in my life. We can know the past but the present is hidden from us. The present will be known by the historians or by the novelists who will call themselves historians. But as to what is happening today, that is part of the general mystery of the universe.

So I have preferred to reread. In Geneva I was taught French, I was taught Latin, and even, as I said in a poem, having forgotten Latin is a possession. And in a sense I am speaking a kind of dog Latin, since I

1

am speaking in Spanish, but I always look back with yearning, a kind of homesickness, for Latin. And this is what so many writers have felt the world over. Samuel Johnson, one of my heroes, attempted, very successfully, to write Latin in English. Quevedo and Saevedra Fejardo and Góngora wrote very fine Latin in Spanish. In a sense we should go back to Latin and we are all doing our best to do so. Forgive the digression of going on and on. In Geneva I taught myself German, because I wanted to read Schopenhauer in the original. And I found a very pleasant way of doing so. I recommend it to all of you if you have no German. The procedure is this. Get hold of a copy of Heine's *Buch der Lieder*—that should be easily done—get hold of a German-English dictionary, and then begin to read. You may be puzzled at first, but after two or three months you will find yourself reading the finest poetry in the world and perhaps not understanding it but feeling it, which is far better, since poetry is not meant for reason but for the imagination.

When I lost my eyesight for reading purposes, I said: This should not be the end. "I will not abound"—as one of the writers I should have mentioned said—"in loud self-pity." No, this should prove the beginning of a new experience. And then I thought: I will explore the language my forefathers spoke. They may have spoken it in Mercia, in Northumbria, now called Northumberland. I will go back to Old English. And so, with a small group, among whom was María Kodama, we began the study of Old English. I know many pieces by heart. Very fine poetry. Not a sentimental line in it. A speech for warriors, for priests, for sailors also, and you find that, some seven centuries after Christ, the English were already looking at the sea. In the early poetry you find the sea around the corner all the time. This happens in England. You find wonderful lines like *on flodes æht   feor gewitan* "to travel far under the power of the ocean." And I have traveled far from the power of the ocean, and here I am, very happily, in the center of your continent, and my continent also, for I am a mere South American. My continent is America.

After that I went on to study Icelandic, and I had already begun that study when I was a boy because my father gave me a copy of the *Volsung Saga* as done into English by William Morris. I enjoyed it greatly and then my father gave me a handbook of Germanic mythology. But the book should really have been called Scandinavian mythology, since Germany, England, the Netherlands, continental Scandinavia had forgotten all about the gods. The memory was kept alive in Iceland. Two years ago I was on a pilgrimage to Iceland—I think William Morris called it the "Holy Land of the North"—but I had already begun that pilgrimage when as a boy I had read Morris' *Volsung Saga* and that handbook of Germanic mythology. Iceland has kept for us the memory of the North. We are all indebted to Iceland. I could hardly tell you what I felt when I landed there. I thought of the sagas, of the eddas. When I was thinking about the eddas, I thought of a poem called "The Greenland Poem." That poem was written or chanted in Greenland by a Norseman; a poem on Attila by the Saxons called "Atle" by the Norseman and "Etzel" by the Germans. I have mentioned Iceland. I have told you the way I felt when I went there, when I saw the men, when I saw those very amiable giants surrounding me. And we talked of course about the sagas and the eddas of the Old North.

I have mentioned this almost secret island. Now I will go on to a second, also secret, island—I suppose all islands are secret. Last year I was in Japan, and I found something quite alien to me. I was, believe it or not, in a very civilized country, an experience which hardly comes to us outside the East. Now, in Japan people have two civilizations—our Western civilization and their own. A man who is a Buddhist can also be a Shintoist, and he may also be a Methodist, as my forefathers were, or a Lutheran, or anything of the kind. People talk about Japanese, or perhaps Chinese, urbanity, but that urbanity goes deep down. I spent some thirty-odd days in Japan. I made many good friends. They never inflicted any anecdotes on me. They told me nothing of their private lives—their lives were indeed private—I told them nothing of mine, and I felt that we were friends because we could talk, not of our mere circumstances, but about real subjects—for example, religion and philosophy.

I have spoken of Iceland, of Japan, now we come, perhaps, to the most secret of all islands, a country I greatly love—it runs in my blood. I'm talking of course of England. I remember what Novalis said: *Jeder Engländer ist eine Insel* "Every Englishman is an island." Of course he is an islander compared to Paris, compared to Buenos Aires. London is a private city, a secret city, and I thoroughly enjoyed it, and I think of the English language and of English literature as being among the greatest adventures of mankind.

Why not speak of another secret island? Why not speak of Manhattan? When one thinks of Manhattan, one thinks of New York as being a public city. Yet you are blinded by it as you are blinded by the sun. The sun of course is secret. Only eagles, we are told, are allowed to look at the sun. And I cannot look on New York, not because I am blind, but because I am blinded by it. At the same time I love it. When I speak of New York, I think instantly of Walt Whitman. Walt Whitman was one of those men who cannot be thought away. And you can say that of many *American* writers. Literature would not be what it is today had there been no Edgar Allan Poe, no Walt Whitman—I mean the myth created by Whitman, not the man himself—no Herman Melville, no Thoreau, and no Emerson. I love Emerson and I am very fond of his poetry. He is to me the one intellectual poet—in any case, the one intellectual poet who has ideas. The others are merely intellectual with no ideas at all. In the case of Emerson he had ideas and was thoroughly a poet. He influenced Emily Dickinson, perhaps the greatest lady writer and the greatest poet that America—I'm thinking of our America also—has as yet produced.

So I have mentioned four islands. I've spoken of Iceland, I've spoken of Japan—I know I'll keep thinking back on Japan all my life—England, and New York. But why should we keep talking about islands? Let us expect a different question and I hope a quite different answer, though I keep saying the same things over and over. I'm an old man, forgive me.

WILLIS BARNSTONE: When Hart Crane wrote "this great wing of eternity" on the typewriter, he realized he had typed by mistake "this great wink of eternity," which was much better, and he left it that way.

BORGES: *Wink* is better than *wing?* No. I don't think so. I don't agree with you. How can you prefer *wink* to *wing?* Oh, look here, you can't go on this way.

BARNSTONE: In any case, Hart Crane made a mistake either on his typewriter or in his judgment, and my question to you is that we make many mistakes—

BORGES: I prefer wings to winks.

BARNSTONE: Mistakes personal, professional, and literary. Some of them lead us to disaster, some to good things.

BORGES: My life has been an encyclopedia of mistakes. A museum.

BARNSTONE: To use Frost's words, which path in the wood do we take? When you took the wrong roads in your life, could you tell us of the disasters or the good things that came as a result?

BORGES: You mean the wrong books I have written?

Barnstone: Yes, and the wrong women you have loved, the wrong days you have spent.

Borges: Yes, but what can I do about it? All those things, the wrong women, the wrong actions, the wrong circumstances, all those are tools to the poet. A poet should think of all things as being given him, even misfortune. Misfortune, defeat, humiliation, failure, those *are* our tools. You don't suppose that when you are happy you can produce anything. Happiness is its own aim. But we are given mistakes, we are given nightmares, almost nightly, and our task is to make them into poetry. And were I truly a poet I would feel that every moment of my life is poetic, every moment of my life is a kind of clay I have to model, I have to shape, to lick into poetry. So that I don't think I should apologize for my mistakes. Those mistakes were given me by that very complex chain of causes and effects, or rather, unending effects and causes—we may not begin by the cause—in order that I might turn them into poetry. And I have a fine tool, the Spanish language, and I have of course the presents of English, the memory of Latin, and another language I greatly love, German. Now I'm studying Old English and doing my best to know something of Japanese, and I hope to go on and on. Of course I know that I am eighty. I hope I may die at any moment, but what can I do about it but to go on living and dreaming, since dreaming is my task? I have to be dreaming all the time, and then those dreams have to become words, and I have to tackle them and do my best or my worst with them. So I don't think I should apologize for my mistakes. As for my own writings, I have never reread them. I don't know them. When I write something it is because I have to. Then once it's published I do my best, very easily, to forget it. Since we are among friends, I will tell you something. When you come to my house—and I hope you all come in due time, to my house on Calle Maipú, on the north side of Buenos Aires—you'll find quite a good library but not a single book of mine, because I don't allow them to have a place in my library. My library is compounded of *good* books. And who am I to be a neighbor to Virgil or Stevenson? So there is no book of mine in my house. You need not fear a single copy.

Oclander: Borges, since you are talking about your house, you are from some place and you've traveled everywhere.

Borges: No, no. Not everywhere. I hope to go to China and to India. I was already there since I've read Kipling and the *Tao Te Ching*.

OCLANDER: Perhaps you could take us where most of us have never been, or will be, where you grew up, in the old Buenos Aires, the streets of Buenos Aires and its history.

BORGES: Really I saw very little of it. I was born in a rather slummy side of the town called Palermo, but it never interested me. I was interested in Palermo in the year '29 or so. But as a boy, my memories are memories of the books I read. Those are far more real to me than the place itself. So that my memories are really memories of Stevenson, of Kipling, and of the *Arabian Nights,* and of *Don Quixote* (I began reading it as a boy, and have gone on reading it, especially the second part, the best I should say. The first part may safely be omitted, perhaps, except for the first chapter, which is really wonderful.) So what can I say about my childhood? But little. I remember pictures of my forefathers, I remember swords that have done service—in what you call the winning of the West and we called *La conquista del desierto,* the conquest of the desert. My grandfather fought the red Indians, or the pampas Indians as we call them—*Los indios pampas.* But I have but few personal memories of that time. My memory is chiefly of books. In fact, I hardly remember my own life. I can give you no dates. I know that I have traveled in some seventeen or eighteen countries, but I can't tell you the order of my travels. I can't tell you how long I was in one place or another. The whole thing is a jumble of division, of images. So that it seems that we are falling back on books. That happens when people speak to me. I always fall back on books, on quotations. I remember that Emerson, one of my heroes, warned us against that. He said: "Let us take care. Life itself may become a long quotation."

BARNSTONE: I would like to ask you about hell.

BORGES: I know it only too well.

BARNSTONE: What is hell? Is doomsday now, at every second? Is it something you find in a nightmare? What does hell mean to you, Borges?

BORGES: Firstly, I'm very glad that my friend has mentioned nightmare, since a nightmare is different from all other dreams. I have read many books on dreams, volumes of psychology, but I have never found anything interesting on nightmares. And yet the nightmare is different from other dreams. The name itself is interesting. I think that etymologically the nightmare may bear two meanings. The nightmare may be the fable of the night. You have the German word *Märchen* akin to it. Or it may be the demon of the night or it may be, for all we know, a mare.

I think Shakespeare speaks of the nightmare, of the nightfold, and Hugo had surely read that because in one of his books—I greatly love Hugo— he speaks of *le cheval noir de la nuit* "the black horse of night," and that of course stands for nightmare. Now, I think the great difference between everyday misfortune and nightmare is that nightmare has a different taste to it. I have been unhappy many times over. Everybody has. I never had the nightmare feeling except when I had the actual nightmare. And we might think—why not? everything is allowed today, and here we are among friends and, though this is very sad to say, I must be sincere to you—that the nightmare is a proof of the existence of hell. In nightmare we feel a very special kind of horror, not felt in any other way as far as I'm aware. Unhappily, I know nightmares only too well, and they have been very helpful to literature. I remember the splendid nightmares—were they dreams or were they inventions? It's all the same—the splendid nightmares of De Quincey, *Confessions of an English Opium Eater.* Also there are many tales of Edgar Allan Poe. You may find that such and such a sentence is wrong or we dislike such and such a metaphor, but they are really nightmares. And of course, in the case of the works of Kafka, you get nightmares also. So as to hell, it may be possible, there may be a state somewhere where all things are nightmare. Let us hope not, since the taste for nightmare is sufficient. It is as keen as physical pain and as unbearable.

As to hell, I suppose hell is not a place. People may think it is because of reading Dante, but I think of it as a state. And I remember part of a verse from Milton, where Satan says: "Myself am Hell." And I was translating, with María Kodama, Angelus Silesius' *Cherubinischer Wandersmann* and we came to the same statement that if a soul is damned it is forever in hell. There is no use in finding its way to heaven. And the great Swedish mystic Swedenborg thought much the same way. The damned are unhappy in hell but would be far unhappier in heaven. And if you want the whole philosophy of Swedenborg in a nutshell, you can find it in the second act of George Bernard Shaw's *Man and Superman,* where the name of Swedenborg is not mentioned, but the whole scheme of heaven and hell is given as being, not a reward or a punishment, but as a state of the soul. A soul finds its way into hell or heaven, or rather becomes hell or heaven through itself. And I find at the close of every day—I'm eighty years old—I am living moments of felicity—

that may be heaven—and moments of unhappiness which we might, by a not too exaggerated metaphor, call hell.

OCLANDER: Borges, you once said that it is the privilege of the blind to see. You have talked about Manhattan, and I think there is an entire part of our audience which has never seen the people and cultures of America . . .

BORGES: There are so many peoples here, and so different.

OCLANDER: Would it be possible for you to talk to us about the United States and the differences in its peoples and its cultures?

BORGES: A very large question. I'm afraid I'm not qualified to answer it. But I can say that I have a very friendly memory of Texas, especially of Austin. I discovered America via Texas in 1961, with my mother, who died at the age of ninety-nine some four or five years ago. I love the South, but since I've mentioned all those writers, I also love the East, and if I think of the Midwest I have to think in terms of Carl Sandburg. I also love him. But the great American poet of this century is Robert Frost. That's the name I would choose. But really I don't think I love things "against" each other. I love all countries and all the writers I have read (and there are many I have never read who are still shedding an influence on me), and I am a disciple of the past, of the whole past. I don't believe in schools. I don't believe in chronology. I don't believe in dating writings. I think poetry should be anonymous. For example, if I could choose I would like a line of mine, a story of mine, rewritten and bettered by somebody else, to survive, and I would wish my personal name to be forgotten, as in due time it will. That happens to all writers. What do we know of the names of the men who wrote that splendid dream, the *Arabian Nights?* We don't and we don't care. What do we know of the private life of Shakespeare? We know nothing and we don't care, since he turned that private life into Macbeth, Hamlet, into the sonnets. Those sonnets are enigmas of course. Swinburne spoke of the sonnets as "those divine and dangerous documents." That's a fine sentence. I wonder whether it's true or not. I think in the case of an author the best thing is to be a part of tradition, to be a part of a language, since the language goes on and the books may be forgotten, or perhaps every age rewrites the same books over and over again, changing or adding a few circumstances. Perhaps the eternal books are all the same books. We are always rewriting what the ancients wrote, and that should prove sufficient.

As to me, personally, I have no ambition. I think that I am a mistake, that people have made too much of me. I am a greatly overrated writer. At the same time I am grateful to you all for taking me seriously. I don't.

BARNSTONE: After hell, by the same reasoning, could you tell us about heaven?

BORGES: I read a book written by an English clergyman saying that there is much sorrow in heaven. I believe so. And I hope so. For, after all, joy is unbearable. We can be happy during a moment or so, but an eternity of happiness is unthinkable. But personally I disbelieve in an afterlife. I hope I shall cease. When I feel sorry, when I am worried—and I am being worried all the time—I say to myself: Why worry when at any moment salvation may come in the shape of annihilation, of death? Since I am about to die, since I may die at any moment, why worry about things? What I am looking for is not utter blackness, for blackness is something after all. No, what I want is to be forgotten—and of course I'll be forgotten. Everything will be forgotten in due time.

OCLANDER: Today you were saying that the hardest voyage of all is the voyage which is about to come, that anticipation is the hardest thing of all. Would you comment?

BORGES: I wonder if I ever said that. What I said was that expecting things was awful. But when things came, the present becomes the past quite soon. It slips into the past. I read a very fine book by Bradley. The book is called *Appearance and Reality* and therein he speaks of time as a river. Well, of course, Heraclitus and all that, Wolfe's *Of Time and the River,* and so on. Bradley thought of time as flowing towards us from the future. We are always swimming against the current. And the moment when the future turns into or melts into the past, this is the present moment. The present is a moment when the future becomes the past. I underwent a very severe and painful operation some six months ago. I stood in fear of it. Then I told myself, this fear, this anticipation, three more days and three more nights to come, all this is part of the operation itself. And then I felt quite lucky about it.

BARNSTONE: You've been immersed in the writings of the gnostics, the mystics, in the Kabbalah, the *Book of Splendor.*

BORGES: I've done my best, but I am very ignorant.

BARNSTONE: You have been interested in the mystics—

BORGES: At the same time I am no mystic myself.

BARNSTONE: I imagine that you would consider the voyage of the mystics a true experience but a secular one. Could you comment on the mystical experience in other writing, in Fray Luis de León . . .

BORGES: I wonder if Fray Luis de León had any mystical experience. I should say not. When I talk of mystics, I think of Swedenborg, Angelus Silesius, and the Persians also. Not the Spaniards. I don't think they had any mystical experiences.

BARNSTONE: John of the Cross?

BORGES: I think that Saint John of the Cross was following the pattern of the Song of Songs. And that's that. I suppose he never had any actual experience. In my life I only had two mystical experiences and I can't tell them because what happened is not to be put into words, since words, after all, stand for a shared experience. And if you have not had the experience you can't share it—as if you were to talk about the taste of coffee and had never tried coffee. Twice in my life I had a feeling, a feeling rather agreeable than otherwise. It was astonishing, astounding. I was overwhelmed, taken aback. I had the feeling of living not in time but outside time. I don't know how long that feeling lasted, since I was outside time. It may have been a minute or so, it may have been longer. But I know that I had that feeling in Buenos Aires, twice in my life. Once I had it on the south side, near the railroad station *Constitución*. Somehow the feeling came over me that I was living beyond time, and I did my best to capture it, but it came and went. I wrote poems about it, but they are normal poems and do not tell the experience. I cannot tell it to you, since I cannot retell it to myself, but I had that experience, and I had it twice over, and maybe it will be granted me to have it one more time before I die.

OCLANDER: Why do you want to travel to China? What do you hope to find there?

BORGES: I feel in a way that I have always been in China. I felt that when I read Herbert Allan Giles' *History of Chinese Literature*. Then I have read and reread many translations of the *Tao Te Ching*. I think the finest one is by Arthur Waley, but I have also read the Wilhelm one and the French translation, and there have been many Spanish translations. Besides, as I spent a month in Japan, in Japan you feel the tutelar ghost of China all the time. This has nothing to do with politics. It has nothing to do with the fact that Japanese culture is a culture of its own.

In Japan people feel China the way we feel Greece. Of course I know I shall never know Chinese, but shall go on reading translations. I read *The Dream of the Red Chamber*. I wonder if you have read it. I have read it in the English and the German translation, but I know that there is a far vaster, and perhaps the strictest, translation into French. *The Dream of the Red Chamber*. The book, I assure you, is as good as its title.

BARNSTONE: Please take us back into the island of consciousness, to the source of words, thought and sensations, and tell us what happens there before language, before the words have been minted by Borges.

BORGES: I think I can say that writing poetry or writing fables—it all boils down to the same thing—is a process beyond one's will. I have never attempted a subject. I have never looked for a subject. I allow subjects to look for me, and then walking down the street, going from one room to another of my house, the small house of a blind man, I feel that something is about to happen, and that something may be a line or it may be some kind of shape. We may take the metaphor of an island. I see two tips. And those tips are the beginning of a poem, the beginning of a fable, and the end. And that's that. And I have to invent, I have to manufacture, what comes in between. That is left to me. What the muse, or the Holy Ghost, to use a finer and a darker name, gives me is the end and the beginning of a story or of a poem. And then I have to fill it in. I may take the wrong path and have to retrace my steps. I have to invent something else. But I always know the beginning and the end. That is my personal experience.

I suppose that every poet has his own method, and there are writers, I am told, who know only the beginning, and they go on, and near the end they discover or they invent—the two words mean the same thing—the ending. But in my case I must know the beginning and the end. And I do my best not to allow my opinions to intrude on what I write. I am not thinking of the moral of the fable but of the fable. Opinions come and go, politics come and go, my personal opinions are changing all the time. But when I write I try to be faithful to the dream, to be true to the dream. That's all I can say. And when I began writing, I wrote in a very baroque style. I did my best to be Sir Thomas Browne or to be Góngora or to be Lugones or to be somebody else. Then I was trying to cheat the reader all the time, always using archaisms or novelties or neologisms. But now I try to write very simple words. I try to avoid, what is called in English, hard words or dictionary words. I do my best to avoid them. And I think that my best book of short stories is the last one I wrote, *El libro de arena, The Book of Sand,* and there I think there is not a single word that may detain the reader or hinder him. The stories are told in a very plain way, though the stories themselves are not plain, since there are no plain things in the universe, since everything is complex. I disguise them as simple stories. In fact, I write, I rewrite them some nine or ten times, and then I want to have the feeling that the whole thing has been done in a rather careless way. I try to be as ordinary as possible. If you don't know my books, there are two books I venture to recommend to your attention. They will take you an hour or so, and that's that. One, a book of poems, called *Historia de la luna, History of the Moon,** and the other, *El libro de arena, The Book of Sand.* As for the rest, you can very easily forget them, and I will be very grateful to you if you do, since I have forgotten them.

BARNSTONE: Death is a marker of time. We have two deaths: before our birth and then after our life is done. These are the public deaths, but perhaps the real personal death is the one we live daily, which we imagine . . .

BORGES: You remember Saint Paul: "I die daily."

BARNSTONE: Death is only something we can perceive now. The mystics speak of death-in-life as an experience outside time. How do you perceive it?

BORGES: I think that one is dying all the time. Every time we are not feeling something, discovering something, when we are merely repeating something mechanically. At that moment you are dead. Life may come at any moment also. If you take a single day, therein you find many deaths, I suppose, and many births also. But I try not to be dead. I try to be curious concerning things, and now I am receiving experiences all the time, and those experiences will be changed into poems, into short stories, into fables. I am receiving them all the time, though I know that many of the things I do and things I say are mechanical, that is to say, they belong to death rather than to life.

OCLANDER: I would like you to take us on a trip to someplace you have not been.

BORGES: I should say that that one place is the past, because it is very difficult to change the present. The present has something hard

---

*Title is actually *Historia de la noche, History of the Night.*

and rigid about it. But as to the past, we are changing it all the time. Every time we remember something, we slightly alter our memory. And I think we should be grateful to the whole past, to the history of mankind, to all the books, to all the memories, since, after all, the only thing we have is the past, and the past is an act of faith. For example I say "I was born in Buenos Aires in 1899." Now that's an act of faith. I can't really remember that. Had my parents told me "You were born in the third century in Timbuktu," I would have believed them of course. But I stick to that fact since I supposed they were not lying to me. So that when I say I was born in Buenos Aires in 1899 I'm really committing an act of faith.

To go back to the past, the past is our treasure. It is the only thing we have, and it is at our disposal. We can change it, think of historical characters as being different, and what is very fine is the fact that the past is compounded not only of things that happened but of things that were dreams. I should say that Macbeth is as much a person of the past and to us a person of the present as, let us say, Charles of Sweden, Julius Caesar, or Bolívar. We have the books, and those books are really dreams, and every time we reread a book that book is slightly different and we are slightly different also. So I think we can fall back safely on that vast emporium, the past. I hope I shall keep on finding my way into it, and add into it my physical experience of life.

2

When I Wake Up

WFIU, Indiana University,
March 1976

When I wake up, I wake to something worse.
It's the astonishment of being myself.

WILLIS BARNSTONE: In case you want a hardboiled egg?

JORGE LUIS BORGES: Why, of course.

BARNSTONE: And I'll crack it for you.

BORGES: Look here, if not, I can't break a hardboiled egg. Not a hardboiled one!

BARNSTONE: It's good to bring hardboiled eggs into radio stations, no?

BORGES: A fine combination, I feel. Hardboiled eggs and radio stations!

BARNSTONE: Borges, would you put them in a poem?

BORGES: No, I wouldn't. Yet I suppose all things are right for a poem. All words are right. In fact, all things are. Anything can be done, you know, but very few things can be talked about.

BARNSTONE: I have some questions. Maybe wordy, but your answers won't be.

BORGES: They will be laconic, yes?

BARNSTONE: We know that consciousness resides in every other human being, yet we possess an awareness of only our own mind. At times we wake, as it were, to a puzzling knowledge of the mind's separate existence.

BORGES: Well, but this is a question on the nature of solipsism, no? Now, I don't believe in solipsism, because if I did I'd go mad. But of course it is a curious fact that we exist.

At the same time, I feel I am not dreaming you, or, let's put it the other way, that you are not dreaming me. But this fact of wondering at life may stand for the essence of poetry. All poetry consists in feeling things as being strange, while all rhetoric consists in thinking of them as quite common, as obvious. Of course I *am* puzzled by the fact of my

15

existing, of my existing in a human body, of my looking through eyes, hearing through ears, and so on. And maybe everything I have written is a mere metaphor, a mere variation on that central theme of being puzzled by things. In that case, I suppose, there's no essential difference between philosophy and poetry, since both stand for the same kind of puzzlement. Except that in the case of philosophy the answer is given in a logical way, and in the case of poetry you use metaphor. If you use language, you have to use metaphors all the time. Since you know my works (well, let the word go at that. I don't think of them as *works,* really), since you know my *exercises,* I suppose you have felt that I was being puzzled all the time, and I was trying to find a foundation for my puzzlement.

BARNSTONE: In Cincinnati when an admirer said "May you live one thousand years," you answered "I look forward happily to my death." What did you mean by that?

BORGES: I mean that when I'm unhappy—and that happens quite often to all of us—I find a real consolation in the thought that in a few years, or maybe in a few days, I'll be dead and then all this won't matter. I look forward to being blotted out. But if I thought that my death was a mere illusion, that after death I would go on, then I would feel very, very unhappy. For, really, I'm sick and tired of myself. Now, of course if I go on and I have no personal memory of ever having been Borges, then in that case it won't matter to me because I may have been hundreds of odd people before I was born, but those things won't worry me, since I will have forgotten them. When I think of mortality, of death, I think of those things in a hopeful way, in an expectant way. I should say I am greedy for death, that I want to stop waking up every morning, finding: Well, here I am, I have to go back to Borges.

There's a word in Spanish, I suppose you know. I wonder if it's any longer in use. Instead of saying "to wake up," you say *recordarse,* that is, to record yourself, to remember yourself. My mother used to say *Que me recuerde a las ocho* "I want to be recorded to myself at eight." Every morning I get that feeling because I am more or less nonexistent. Then when I wake up, I always feel I'm being let down. Because, well, here I am. Here's the same old stupid game going on. I have to be somebody. I have to be exactly that somebody. I have certain commitments. One of the commitments is to live through the whole day. Then I see all that routine before me, and all things naturally make me tired. Of course when you're young, you don't feel that way. You feel, well, I am so glad I'm back in this marvelous world. But I don't think I ever felt that way. Even when I was young. Especially when I was young. Now I have resignation. Now I wake up and I say: I have to face another day. I let it go at that. I suppose that people feel in different ways because many people think of immortality as a kind of happiness, perhaps because they don't realize it.

BARNSTONE: They don't realize what?

BORGES: The fact that going on and on would be, let's say, awful.

BARNSTONE: Would be another hell, as you say in one of your stories.

BORGES: Yes, it would be, yes. Since this life is already hell, why go in for more and more hell, for larger and larger doses!

BARNSTONE: For two hundred years?

BORGES: Yes. Well, of course you might say that those two hundred years don't exist. For what really exists is the present moment. The present moment is being weighted down by the past and by the fear of the future. Really, when do we speak of the present moment? For the present moment is as much an abstraction as the past or the future. In the present moment, you always have some kind of past and some kind of future also. You are slipping all the time from one to the other.

BARNSTONE: But obviously you have great moments of pleasure during your life.

BORGES: Yes, I suppose everybody has. But I wonder. I suppose those moments are perhaps finer when you remember them. Because when you're happy, you're hardly conscious of things. The fact of being conscious makes for unhappiness.

BARNSTONE: To be conscious of happiness often lets in an intrusion of doubt.

BORGES: But I think I have known moments of happiness. I suppose all men have. There are moments, let's say, love, riding, swimming, talking to a friend, let's say, conversation, reading, even *writing*, or rather, not writing but inventing something. When you sit down to write it, then you are no longer happy because you're worried by technical problems. But when you think out something, then I suppose you may be allowed to be happy. And there are moments when you're slipping into sleep, and then you feel happy, or at least I do. I remember the first time I had sleeping pills. (They were efficient, of course, since they were new to me.) I used to say to myself: Now hearing that tramway turn around the corner, I won't be able to hear the end of the noise it makes, the rumble, because

I'll be asleep. Then I felt very, very happy. I thought of unconsciousness.

BARNSTONE: Do you care about literary recognition? Do you want fame?

BORGES: No. No! Those things are nonexistent. At the same time, when it comes to me—and it may have come to me—I feel that I should be grateful. I mean if people take me seriously, I think, well, they are wrong. At the same time I should be thankful to them.

BARNSTONE: Do you live for the next poem, story, or essay or conversation?

BORGES: Yes. Yes, I do.

BARNSTONE: It seems to me that you're a lucky man to have unending obsessions to create and to record. Do you know why you had that destiny of being a writer? That destiny or that obsession?

BORGES: The only thing I know is that I need those obsessions. Because if not, why should I go on living? Of course I wouldn't commit suicide. But I should feel very unjustified. This doesn't mean I think very much of what I write. It means that I *have* to write. Because if I don't write something and keep on being obsessed by it, then I have to write it and be rid of it.

BARNSTONE: In the *Republic,* Plato spends much time seeking a definition of justice, a kind of public definition. Is this notion valid to us personally? Is your life, which ends in death, a just experiment in life, or is it a biological doublecross against both the mind and the body? Plato speaks about public justice. Given the fact of death, do you believe in private justice?

BORGES: I think that the only justice is private justice because, as to a public justice, I wonder if that really exists.

BARNSTONE: Do you believe private justice exists? How do we consider morality and doomsday?

BORGES: At the very moment of our lives we know whether we're acting the right way or the wrong way. We might say that doomsday is going on all the time, that every moment of our lives we're acting wrongly or rightly. Doomsday is not something that comes at the end. It's going on all the time. And we know, through some instinct, when we have acted rightly or wrongly.

BARNSTONE: Is there a biological treason in life because of death?

BORGES: I don't understand what you mean by biological doublecross. Biology sounds so dim to me, I wonder if I can take that word in, no?

BARNSTONE: *Physical,* then.

BORGES: Well, *physical,* yes. I think I can understand that. I am a very simpleminded man. If you go in for those long fancy words, *biology* and *psychology*—

BARNSTONE: We get into language that your father might have used, right?

BORGES: Yes, he might have used it, but he rarely did so, being a professor of psychology, a skeptic also.

BARNSTONE: I spent one year of my life, when I was a student, seeking the center of consciousness. I never found it.

BORGES: I don't think you can. It keeps eluding you all the time.

BARNSTONE: But I did discover that seeking oneself was fascinating and intolerable.

BORGES: Yes, it is. Of course since I am blind, I have to do that more or less all the time. Before I went blind, I was always finding refuge in watching things, seeing things, in reading, while now I have to go in for thinking or, since my thinking capacity isn't too good, let's say for dreaming, and in a sense for dreaming away my life. That's the only thing I can do. Then of course I have to go in for long spells of loneliness, but I don't mind that. Before, I couldn't. Before, I remember I lived in a town called Adrogué south of Buenos Aires. When I went on a half hour's journey and I had no book with me I felt very unhappy. But now I can spend hours and hours on end, with no books, because I don't read them. And so I don't think of loneliness as being necessarily unhappy. Or, for example, if I get a spell of insomnia, I don't mind about it because time slips down. It's like an easy slope, no? So I just let myself go on living. Now, when I was not blind, I always had to be furnishing my time with different things. Now I don't. I just let myself go.

BARNSTONE: Yet you do very much enjoy all the times you are with others.

BORGES: But of course, I live in memory. And I suppose a poet should live in memory because, after all, what is imagination? Imagination, I should say, is made of memory and of oblivion. It is a kind of blending of the two things.

BARNSTONE: You manage with time?

BORGES: Oh yes. Everybody who goes blind gets a kind of reward: a different sense of time. Time is no longer to be filled in at every moment by something. No. You know that you have just to live on, to let time live you. That makes for a certain comfort. I think it is a great comfort, or perhaps a great reward. A gift of blindness is that you feel time in a different way from most people, no? You have to remember and you have to forget. You shouldn't remember everything because, well, the character I wrote about, Funes, goes mad because his memory is endless. Of course if you forgot everything, you would no longer exist. Because you exist in your past. Otherwise you wouldn't even know who you were, what your name was. You should go in for a blending of the two elements, no? Memory and oblivion, and we call that imagination. That's a high-sounding name.

BARNSTONE: I know you don't go in for high-sounding words because you're a literary man.

BORGES: No, because I am too skeptical about words. A literary man hardly believes in words.

BARNSTONE: To return to my original question: As I attempted to discover myself, it was fascinating and intolerable because the more profoundly I thought I had gone into myself, the more I disappeared until I was uncertain of everything, even of my own existence.

BORGES: Well, I think Hume said, when I've looked for myself I have never found anybody at home. That's the way the world is.

BARNSTONE: One goes from reverie to nightmare.

BORGES: I have a nightmare almost every night. I had one this morning. But it wasn't a real nightmare.

BARNSTONE: What was it?

BORGES: It was this: I found myself in a very large building. It was a brick building. Many empty rooms. Large empty rooms. Brick rooms. Then I went from one to the other, and there seemed to be no doors. I was always finding my way into courtyards. Then after a time I was going up and down, I was calling out, and there was nobody. That large and unimaginative building was empty, and I said to myself: Why, of course, this is the dream of the maze. So I won't find any door, so I'll just have to sit down in one of the rooms and then wait. And sometimes I wake up. And that actually happened. When I realized it and said, this is the nightmare of the maze, and since I knew all about it, I wasn't taken in by the maze. I merely sat down on the floor.

BARNSTONE: And waited it out.

BORGES: I waited a moment and woke up.

BARNSTONE: You have other recurrent nightmares? What are they?

BORGES: I have two or three. At this moment I think the maze is the one that comes back to me. Then I have another one, and that came out of my blindness. That is a nightmare of trying to read and of being unable to because the characters become alive, because every letter turns into other letters, and then the words at the beginning are short when I try to make them out. They are long Dutch words with repeated vowels. Or, if not, the spaces between the lines widen out, and then the letters are branching out, and all that is done in black or red characters, on very glossy paper, and so large as to be intolerable. And when I wake up, those characters keep me company for some time. Then for a wild moment I think: I'll never be able to forget them and I'll go mad. That seems to be happening all the time. Especially after I lost my sight, I was having that dream of reading, of being unable to read because of the characters becoming alive. That is one of the dreams I have. And the others are dreams about mirrors, about masked people. I suppose I have three essential nightmares: the maze, the writing, and the mirrors. And then there are others that are more or less common to everybody, but those are my three recurrent nightmares. I have them almost every night. They stay with me for a minute or so after I'm awake. Sometimes they come before I'm quite asleep. Most people dream before going to sleep, and then they keep on dreaming a moment after they awake. They are in a kind of halfway house, no? Between waking and sleeping.

BARNSTONE: It's also a place from which you gather much material for your writing, isn't it?

BORGES: Yes, it is. De Quincey and so on. There is a fine literary tradition to that. De Quincey must have worked out his nightmares when he wrote them down, no? Because they're so fine. Besides, they depend on words also. While nightmares, generally, don't depend on words. What's difficult about writing a nightmare is that the nightmare feeling does not come from the images. Rather, as Coleridge said, the feeling gives you the images.

BARNSTONE: That's a major distinction, because most people think the opposite. They don't think it all through.

BORGES: When you write down the images, those images may not mean anything to you. It's what you get in the case of Poe and of Lovecraft. The images are awful but the feeling isn't awful.

BARNSTONE: And I suppose a good writer is one who comes up with the right images to correspond to the feeling.

BORGES: To a feeling, yes. Or who may give you the nightmare feeling with common objects or things. I remember how I found a proof of that in Chesterton. He says that we might think that at the end of the world there is a tree whose very shape is evil. Now that's a fine word, and I think that stands for that kind of feeling, no? Now, that tree could hardly be described. While, if you think of a tree, for example, made of skulls, of ghosts, that would be quite silly. But what we said, a tree *whose very shape* is evil. That shows he really had a nightmare about that tree. No? If not, how would he know about that tree?

BARNSTONE: I've always been puzzled why my tongue moves, why words come out of my mouth or from in my head. These words are like seconds of a clock, happening, sounding almost by themselves.

BORGES: But I think that before going to sleep you begin, at least I begin, to mumble meaningless sentences. And then I know that I am going to sleep. When I hear myself, when I overhear myself saying something meaningless, it's a good sign that I'll be asleep in a moment.

BARNSTONE: Well, I was going to ask you, about the words happening, forming in our mouths. As long as time exists, the words come. Hence also the thoughts. But I don't will those words, or even will to will them. They possess me.

BORGES: I don't think those words stand for any meaning. At least you don't know the meaning.

BARNSTONE: I don't mean the words before one sleeps. I mean all the words that are coming to you right this moment or to me. In other words, I don't know why words are coming out of my mouth right now. Some force is letting them out. I am never there manipulating them. I don't understand that. It's a kind of fundamental mystery to me.

BORGES: But I suppose those words go with certain thoughts. But otherwise they would be meaningless or irrelevant.

BARNSTONE: But I feel like a clock wound up in which the seconds tick, in which words come. I have no idea why I'm speaking to you in any half logical way now. Or why you're answering me. It's a tremendous puzzle to me.

BORGES: Yes. I think you should accept that.

BARNSTONE: I do accept it or I'd go mad.

BORGES: Yes, that's it. You might even say that if you try to think, you go mad.

BARNSTONE: Yes.

BORGES: Thought should be carefully avoided, right?

BARNSTONE: Well, if you try to think why you think, you can't think that. Yet sometimes I walk down the street and say, not who is this walking down the street, but who is this thinking he's walking down the street, and then I'm really puzzled.

BORGES: Yes, and then you go on to thinking who is this thinking he's thinking he's thinking, no? I don't think that stands for anything. That's merely grammatical, they are only words.

BARNSTONE: It sounds like a mirror.

BORGES: You might go into a second category. You may feel a very strong physical pain. For example, you may get it through electricity or through a toothache. Then when you feel that pain, you won't feel the pain. Then after that you say, well, this is a toothache, and then you know that you felt the pain. Then after that you might go for a third time and say, well, I knew that I knew. But after that I don't think you can go on. You can do it successfully within the same game, because you keep on thinking the same thing over and over again. But I don't think you could do that any more than three times over. If you say, I think that I think that I think that I think that I think that I think, all of that is quite unreal after the second term, perhaps. I read a book, by John William Dunne, *Experience with Time,* in which he says that since, if you know something, you know that you know it, and you know that you know that you know, and you know that you know, that you know that you know it, then there is an infinity of selves in every man. But I don't think that can be proved.

BARNSTONE: What do you think of that momentary wakening, which is both exhilarating and frightening, of wondering how our minds happen to be thinking and talking? I always wake to the astonishment that I exist, that I am.

BORGES: When I wake up, I wake to something worse. It's the astonishment of being myself. So and so born in Buenos Aires in 1899, somebody who was in Geneva.

BARNSTONE: Why aren't you the Peking Man, or someone who's going to live five million years from now?

BORGES: Well, once I thought out a kind of fantasy, which was for literary purposes. This is that at any moment we all change into somebody else. Now, since you are changed into someone else, you are not aware of it. For example, at some moment I will be changed into you. You will be changed into me. But since the change, the shift, is complete, you have no memories, you don't know that you are changing. You're changing all the time, you may be the man in the moon, yet will not know about it, since, when you became the man in the moon, you became the man in the moon with *his* past, with his memories, with his fears, with his hopes, and so on.

BARNSTONE: The past self is obliterated.

BORGES: Yes, you may be changed into somebody else all the time and nobody would know. Maybe that kind of thing is happening. It would be meaningless, of course. It reminds me of a story, only a story, but things are only good for literary purposes! But for not too good literary purposes, for trick stories.

BARNSTONE: There is a powerful force, always in us, to move out from ourselves to reach the world. It shows itself in all ways: sexually, by writing, by talking, by touching—

BORGES: Well, living.

BARNSTONE: By living. We are only ourselves and yet there exists the strongest impulse to destroy our solitude by including more in it. Sappho has a fragment where she sums it up. She says: "I could not hope/ to touch the sky/ with my two arms." Her thought represents that compelling life force to reach out.

BORGES: If I understand you, you say that we're running away from ourselves all the time, and that we have to do so.

BARNSTONE: We're trying to expand to be more, to reach, to touch outside our own circle.

BORGES: I suppose we are. But I don't think you should worry about that. You should not feel unhappy about that. Though you know we can't do it, or can't do it utterly, only in an imperfect way.

BARNSTONE: We cannot do it, but part of the art of living is to go through the motions of doing it, and it makes for writing, it makes for love, it makes for all the things that bind people together.

BORGES: Since we're given—what?—threescore years and ten, and we have to furnish them somehow, why not attempt those things? And after all, we have a life span. If not, you'd be utterly bored.

BARNSTONE: You obviously value your future work as more important than earlier achievements.

BORGES: Well, I have to.

BARNSTONE: Anything less would be fatal. Yet I'm surprised that you seem to consider your recent books of poems as less important than earlier books of poems.

BORGES: I know them only too well.

BARNSTONE: I'm convinced that your new poems are your most

powerful, in both their intelligence and their passion. The latter is often expressed in a personal despair you do not allow in your stories or essays.

BORGES: No, I think that you are wrong. You think of my poems as being good. You read them through the light of the early poems, but had these poems come to your notice as being the work of an unknown poet, you'd toss them away. Don't you think so? When you read something written by a writer whose work you know, then you read those last pieces as the last pages in a long novel, but those pages would make no sense without the pages that came before them. When you think of a poet, you always tend to think of his last poem as a fine poem, but taken by itself it may not be.

BARNSTONE: Yes, but the last poems also help the early poems because they contribute to the cumulative personality of the voice. Without those last poems your earlier poems would be heard less fully.

BORGES: Well, I suppose they are helping each other.

BARNSTONE: Because they create one total voice. When Blake says something amusing, it's partly amusing because usually he doesn't say anything amusing, and therefore we say: Ah, there's Blake being witty in an epigram.

BORGES: He's generally long-winded and ponderous!

BARNSTONE: To me your new poems are your most powerful in terms of intellect and passion.

BORGES: Let's hope so. I don't think of them in that way. They are mere exercises. Besides, as I feel lonely for something, I feel homesick, those poems are merely experiments in being back in Buenos Aires or in running away from things. They are merely meant to be used for padding the new book I'm writing. But I do hope you're right.

BARNSTONE: As you stand before a mirror or record a dream in the poems, your precise delineation of pathos is a quality lost to modern poetry. It is well that you do not overesteem your recent poems, but you should know that you're probably wrong in your judgment.

BORGES: But I hope I'm wrong! I'm glad to be convinced by you, only I can't. I don't want to be right. Why should I be right? Why should I insist on the fact that I'm writing very poor stuff?

BARNSTONE: Is there a poem usually lurking in your mind that you stumble on? Is it an act of recognition of a common thing, as when you suddenly remember that you love your mother or father? Is it that you fall upon a poem, or does the poem fall on you?

BORGES: I would say the poem falls on me, and even more in the case of a short story. Then I am possessed. Then I have to get rid of it, and the only way to get rid of it is to write it down. There is no other way of doing so, or else it keeps on.

BARNSTONE: You say your poems are mere exercises, but what are they exercises in?

BORGES: I suppose they are exercises in language. They are exercises in the Spanish language, in the euphony of verse, exercises in rhyming also. Since I'm not too good a rhymer, I try to get away with it. And they are also exercises in imagination. In the case of a story, I know that I must think out a story, clearly and coherently, and then I can write it down. If not, I can't. If not, the whole thing would be a jumble of words. It should be more than that. A story should mean not only the words but something behind the words. I remember reading—maybe it was one of Stevenson's essays: "What is a character in a book? A character in a book is merely a string of words," he said. Now, I think that's wrong. He may be a string of words, but he should not leave us the impression of being a string of words. Because when we think of Macbeth or Lord Jim or Captain Ahab, we think of those characters as existing beyond the written words. We are not told everything about them, but there are many things that have happened to them that surely existed. For example, we are told about a character doing such and such a thing. Then the next day he does another thing. Now, the writer doesn't say anything about it. We feel that he had his nights of sleep, that he has had his dreams, that things happened to him that we are not being told about. We think of Don Quixote as having been a child, though there is not a word concerning Don Quixote's childhood in the book, as far as I remember. So the character should be more than a string of words. And if he is not more than words, he would not be a real character. You wouldn't be interested in him. Even in the case of a character who exists, let's say, within ten lines: "Alas, poor Yorick, I knew him well, Horatio." That character exists by himself. Yet he only exists as a string of words within ten lines, or perhaps even less.

BARNSTONE: And in someone else's mouth. He never even presents himself on stage.

BORGES: Yes, in someone else's mouth, and yet you think of him as having been a real man.

BARNSTONE: And feel compassion for him.

BORGES: And feel compassion for him. Shakespeare had Hamlet in a graveyard. He thought that making him handle a skull, a white skull— Hamlet was in black—all that would have made a quite effective picture. But since he couldn't be holding the skull and not saying a word, he had to say something. And so, Yorick came into being through that technical necessity of Shakespeare's. And he came into being forever. In that sense Yorick is far more than a string of words. I suppose Stevenson knew all that, since he was a writer, since he created many characters, and those characters were far more than a string of words.

BARNSTONE: And in ten words he outsmarts time forever.

BORGES: Yes, that's very strange, eh?

BARNSTONE: I have a very personal question.

BORGES: The only interesting questions are personal questions. Not those of the future of the Republic, the future of America, the future of the cosmos! These things are meaningless.

BARNSTONE: I think these questions have all been rather personal.

BORGES: They should be personal.

BARNSTONE: Do you have paternal feelings toward your friends? Or is this word *paternal* completely irrelevant?

BORGES: No, they're not paternal . . .

BARNSTONE: Everyone is an equal?

BORGES: Brotherly, fraternal, rather than paternal. Of course being an old man I'm expected to be paternal, but really I'm not. Now, Macedonio Fernández thought that paternal feelings were wrong. He said to me: "What do I have in common with my son? We belong to different generations. I'm fond of him, but that's my mistake. He's fond of me, that's his mistake. We shouldn't really care for each other." Then I said to him: Yes, that doesn't depend on the rule. You may care for him in spite of those arguments. And suppose that your arguments are made because you think that you are worrying too much over him, or you feel that you haven't done right by him. There's quite a lot of nonsense about fathers not being allowed to love their sons and sons not being allowed to love their fathers.

BARNSTONE: Go on.

BORGES: Of course he had abandoned his family. There's a very obvious explanation: the fact that he had left them to live his own life.

BARNSTONE: To go from fathers to reverie, you speak much of dream. What do you mean by dream? How is a dream different from any other state of wakefulness?

BORGES: Because a dream is a creation. Of course wakefulness may be a creation: part of our solipsism and so on. But you don't think of it in that way. In the case of a dream, you know that all that comes from yourself, whereas, in the case of a waking experience, many things may come to you that don't come out of yourself, unless you believe in solipsism. Then you are the dreamer all the time, whether waking or sleeping. I don't believe in solipsism. I don't suppose anybody really does. The essential difference between the waking experience and the sleeping or dreaming experience must lie in the fact that the dreaming experience is something that can be begotten by you, created by you, evolved out of you.

BARNSTONE: But not necessarily in sleep.

BORGES: No, no, not necessarily in sleep. When you're thinking out a poem, there is little difference between the fact of being asleep and that of being awake, no? And so they stand for the same thing. If you're thinking, if you're inventing, or if you're dreaming, then the dream may correspond to vision or to sleep. That hardly matters.

BARNSTONE: Like all of us, you are a selfish man. You have dwelled on yourself, have explored and exploited your own mind, and have transmitted your observations to others.

BORGES: Well, what else can I do? I shouldn't be blamed, I shouldn't be held to blame for that.

BARNSTONE: Because you have transmitted your self-observations to others, you are surely not selfless. Yet the fact of giving your work to others, as you also offer a kind of Socratic conversation to others, is an act of generosity of a curiously rare ethical breed.

BORGES: I think I need it, because I'm enjoying it also.

BARNSTONE: Yet I fear that this breed of ethical generosity is becoming extinct and that one like you, protected by blindness and loyalty to earlier authors, may not appear again. Then I worry a bit more and become optimistic and think that this ethical man and artist will occur again.

BORGES: He or she will be lost forever and ever!

BARNSTONE: Are you an ethical man?

BORGES: Yes, I am essentially ethical. I always think of things in terms of right and wrong. I think that many people in my country, for example, have little feeling for ethics. I suppose in America people are more ethical than in my country. People here, for example, generally think of a thing as being right or wrong, the war in Viet Nam, and so on. But in my country you think of something as being profitable or unprofitable. That may be the difference. But here Puritanism, Protestantism, all that makes for ethical considerations, while the Catholic religion makes for pomp and circumstance only, that is, for essential atheism.

Barnstone: There's a lot of fun in you, Borges. You're very childlike, you enjoy things, you have a tremendous humor.

Borges: Well, I should, after all. I wonder if I'm really grown up. I don't suppose anybody is.

Barnstone: No, none of us is. When I was unhappy in the past, in love, some foolish things like that—

Borges: No, not foolish. Those things are a part of every human experience. I mean the fact of loving and not being loved, that is a part of every biography, no? But if you came to me and said: I am in love with so-and-so, she's rejected me. I think that every human being can say that. Everyone has been rejected, and has rejected also. Both things stand out in everyone's life. Someone is turning down someone or being turned down. It's happening all the time. Of course when it happens to us, as Heine said, then we're very unhappy.

Barnstone: Sometimes when I was unhappy I wanted to die, but I knew that this was just a sign that I wanted to live.

Borges: I have thought of suicide many times, but I've always put it off. I say, why should I worry, since I have that very powerful weapon, suicide, and at the same time I never used it, at least I don't think I ever used it!

Barnstone: Well, you've almost answered my question. I wanted to say that the thought of suicide was merely a sign of wanting to live, that even the false suicide I often conceived was a desperate wish to live, more fully, better.

Borges: When people think of suicide, they only think of what people will think about them knowing that they committed suicide. So in a sense they go on living. They do it out of revenge, generally speaking. Many people commit suicide because they are angry. It is a way of showing their anger and revenge. To make someone else guilty for what you do, which is remarkably wrong.

Barnstone: Suicide is largely a young man's romance, a false door young people sometimes step into. But what about the converse? Why the passion to live? Why that passion that drives the young to death and the writer to his pen? Why the consuming passion to live?

BORGES: If I could answer that, I could explain the riddle of the universe, and I don't think I can, no? Since everybody else has failed. I've known many suicides. Many of my friends have committed suicide. In fact, among literary men in my country, suicide is fairly common, perhaps more than in this country. But I think that most of them have done it out of a desire to spite somebody, to make somebody guilty of their own death. In most cases that is the motivation. In the case of Leopoldo Lugones, I think he was trying to turn somebody else into a murderer.

BARNSTONE: Sometimes there's a weariness, a desire to be released, when people are very sick.

BORGES: Of course there's another kind of suicide. When a friend of mine knew he had a cancer, he committed suicide, which was a reasonable thing to do. I wouldn't hold that against anybody. I think that it was right.

BARNSTONE: I don't have any more questions unless you have a question you'd like to ask me.

BORGES: No, I would like to thank you for your kindness and for this very pleasant conversation, because I thought of it as an ordeal, and it hasn't been an ordeal. On the contrary, it has been a very pleasant experience. You were very generous to be feeding me, giving me your own thoughts, pretending that I really thought them out. You've done everything, been handling me very deftly all the time, and I'm very grateful to you. Thank you, Barnstone.

BARNSTONE: Thank you, Borges.

3

It Came Like a Slow
Summer Twilight

The Dick Cavett Show,
New York, May 1980

As I found out that I was blind very gradually, there was no special affected moment. It came like a slow summer twilight. I was head librarian of the National Library and I began to find that I was ringed in by letterless books. Then my friends lost their faces. Then I found out there was nobody in the looking glass.

DICK CAVETT: It's nice to have, not only such an eminent poet and writer, but a poultry inspector on the program. Could you explain—it sounds like something out of S. J. Perelman—why you were a chicken inspector?

JORGE LUIS BORGES: I had a small job in a library in Buenos Aires. Then I was given the order to go and inspect the sale of poultry and eggs in markets. I went to the municipality, the town hall, and asked a friend: "Why on earth?" He said: "Well, but you are in favor of the Allies." Of course I was. Then he said: "What could you expect? That's that." Then I said: "Well, of course I can't answer that argument." That was the reason.

CAVETT: And this was the Perón regime.

BORGES: Yes, it was on the side of Hitler and Mussolini. I love Italy and love Germany, and because I do, I loathe Mussolini and Hitler.

CAVETT: How serious an enemy were you of the Peróns? That seems like a sort of an insult, but not a very serious thing to do to you, to make you a poultry inspector. But your mother got a phone call one night that was ominous. Can you tell about that?

BORGES: Yes, she got a phone call in the small hours. I heard the phone call. Then the morning after, I asked her: "Did I dream a phone

33

call?" She said: "No, you haven't. Some fool or other called me and said: 'I am going to kill you, and to kill your son.'" And my mother said: "Killing my son is easy, you can find him any day you like. As for killing me, I am over ninety. You'd better be in a hurry. If you are not I'll die on you." After this she went to sleep.

CAVETT: I'd like to meet her. Has your mother died since then?

BORGES: Yes, my mother died five years ago. She was ninety-nine. At the time, she felt sorry, no? I mean, she said: "Well, this is too much." To live to be ninety-nine is really awful.

CAVETT: Is awful.

BORGES: Yes. Well, to live to be eighty is awful. Living is awful, let's say. But you cannot avoid it. It can be very beautiful. Now, for example, it is beautiful.

CAVETT: Now is okay?

BORGES: Yes, of course. I'm in New York. I'm talking to you.

CAVETT: You like New York.

BORGES: Yes. I think of New York in terms of Walt Whitman, of O. Henry, and also in terms of sheer beauty. The whole city—skyscrapers springing up like fountains. It's a very lyric city.

CAVETT: Señor Borges, is your blindness hereditary?

BORGES: Yes. I saw my father die blind and smiling. My paternal grandmother, she was North Country. She came from Northumberland. I saw her die blind and smiling. And my great-grandfather also died blind. I don't know whether he smiled or not. That's as far back as I can go. I stand in the fourth generation.

CAVETT: How does it change you when you do become blind?

BORGES: As I found out that I was blind very gradually, there was no special affected moment. It came like a slow summer twilight. I was head librarian of the National Library and I began to find that I was ringed in by letterless books. Then my friends lost their faces. Then I found out there was nobody in the looking glass. And then things grew dim, and now I can make out white and gray. But two colors are forbidden me: black and red. I see black and red as brown. Where Shakespeare said "Looking on darkness which the blind do see," he was wrong. The blind are forbidden darkness. I live in the center of a luminous mist.

CAVETT: A luminous mist.

BORGES: Grayish, or bluish, I'm not too sure. It's far too dim. I would say that now I live in the center of a bluish world.

CAVETT: Bluish.

BORGES: But it may be gray for all I know.

CAVETT: Did you try to read everything you could as fast as you could when you knew you were going blind?

BORGES: No. I should have done that, of course. Since then—that was 1955, the year of a revolution—I have done much rereading but little reading.

CAVETT: By braille, and people reading to you?

BORGES: No, I've never attempted braille. But I keep on reading the same books I read when I was a child.

CAVETT: You like *Huck Finn* but not *Tom Sawyer* as I recall.

BORGES: I think that Tom Sawyer spoils the book. Why was he allowed to intrude into the book? *Huckleberry Finn* is a great book.

CAVETT: You mean his appearance at the end of *Huck Finn*.

BORGES: Yes, I think the book falls to pieces. It is such a wonderful book, it can't fall to pieces. It is my personal theory that another great book was begotten by *Huckleberry Finn*. I mean, of course, Kipling's *Kim*. Though the books are totally different—one of them is from America and the other is from India—they have the same scheme, the same framework: an old man and a boy discovering their country. The countries and the style are quite different. Kipling actually met Mark Twain. I read it in one of his books.

CAVETT: And you would have liked to have met both of them.

BORGES: Of course. That book of Kipling's is called *From Sea to Sea,* though I'm not sure. He saw Mark Twain but he never met Robert Louis Stevenson.

CAVETT: He wanted to.

BORGES: Yes, he wanted to, but he never made it.

CAVETT: Sometimes I think you would have been happier being born back a little farther because your fondness for that period is so great.

BORGES: I think of myself as *not* being a modern writer. I'm a nineteenth-century writer. My novelties are nineteenth-century novelties. I don't think of myself as a contemporary of surrealism, or dadaism, or imagism, or the other respected tomfooleries of literature, no? I think of literature in terms of the nineteenth century and the early twentieth century. I am a lover of Bernard Shaw, Henry James.

CAVETT: Your fans are so totally addicted to your work, it's wonderful. I only discovered it, I'm sorry to say, recently. One of the things that one finds immediately is that your work is full of mazes and puzzles and even hoaxes.

BORGES: Well, hoaxes. But mazes are to be explained by the fact that I live in a wonderful world. I mean, I am baffled all the time by things. I am astonished at things.

CAVETT: I know you have talked about Spanish as your doom. That it's a language that limits you so in writing. What is an example of the things that you can't say in Spanish that you can in English?

BORGES: Well, I think I can quote some verses out of "The Battle of East and West" by Kipling. There is an English officer who is pursuing an Afghan horse thief. They are both on horseback and Kipling says: "They have ridden the low moon out of the sky. Their hooves drum up the dawn." Now, you can't ride the low moon out of the sky in Spanish, and you can't drum up the dawn. Those things are not allowed you in Spanish. But in Spanish, of course, we have other virtues. For example, the open vowels. When you spoke Old English you had the open vowels. I think Shakespeare had them also. I was told in Scotland that Shakespeare would actually have said: "Tow be or not tow be, that is the question. Whether 'tis nobler in the maend to suffer the slings and arrows of outrageous fortune."

CAVETT: You hear all those languages. Dim is a beautiful word.

BORGES: It is akin to the German *Dämmerung* "the twilight." *Dämmerung* and *dim,* they go together.

CAVETT: Is there a line about "death's dim vagueless night" in Shakespeare?

BORGES: Of course there is. There you get the Saxon alliteration. And yet alliteration is practically unknown in Spanish. There is a fine verse by Leopoldo Lugones where you hear the *n* sound twice over: *Iba el silencio andando como un largo lebrel.** There you hear alliteration. But that is hardly ever tried in Spanish. We go in for rhyme and assonance, rather.

CAVETT: Have you ever tried writing in English?

BORGES: Yes, but I respect the English language too much. I wrote two or three poems for friends, and they found their way into print, but now I won't attempt it. I do what I can with Spanish. After all, Spanish is my destiny and my tool also. It's my mother tongue.

*"Silence was moving like a long greyhound."

CAVETT: How can you explain something that's always puzzled me, the sympathy for Nazis and Hitler in Argentina?

BORGES: Look here. I think the Argentine Republic cannot be explained. It is as mysterious as the universe. I do not understand it. I don't profess to understand my country. I am not politically minded either. I do my best to avoid politics. I belong to no party. I am an individualist. My father was a student of Herbert Spencer. He was brought up on "man versus the state." I can't explain that kind of thing. I don't understand it myself.

CAVETT: You wrote about Hitler somewhere that you saw him as a man who wanted to lose, in some way.

BORGES: Yes, but maybe the whole thing was a literary game of mine. And yet since people admire Napoleon, why shouldn't they admire Hitler? I think that they go together. If you admire conquerors, you endorse conquerors yourself. But of course I hate and loathe him. His anti-Semitism was very foolish.

CAVETT: The mazes and the labyrinths and the strange patterns that you write in your work, are they there as artistic flourishes or are they there because they are something alive?

BORGES: No. I think of them as essential tokens, as essential symbols. I have not chosen them. They were given me. I stick to them because I find that they are the right symbols for my state of mind. I am always being baffled, perplexed, so a maze is the right symbol. They are not, at least to me, literary devices or tricks. I don't think of them as tricks. They are part of my destiny, of my way of feeling, of living. I haven't chosen them.

CAVETT: Do you still go to movies?

BORGES: Yes, but I can only hear the voices.

CAVETT: I was surprised to hear of your interest in movies and that, in fact, I think you wrote a script once.

BORGES: I remember very fine movies that seem to have been forgotten now. Those movies on gangsters by Joseph von Sternberg. Movies I remember: *The Showdown, The Dragnet.* The actors were George Bancroft, William Powell, Fred Kohler. That was the last of the silent movies. Then you had the talkies and the whole thing changed. I have seen many times over that very fine film *Citizen Kane.*

CAVETT: That's one that people see over and over.

BORGES: And I was frightened to death by *Psycho.* I saw it three or four times over and I knew the moment I had to close my eyes in order not to see the mother.

CAVETT: You said somewhere that unhappiness is a blessing for the writer.

BORGES: I should say that unhappiness is one of the many tools given to the writer. Or one of the many materials, for another metaphor. Unhappiness, solitude, all those should be used by the writer. Even the nightmare is a tool. Many of my stories have been given me by nightmares. I have a nightmare every other night.

CAVETT: What is the story in which no one ages? After a certain point no one dies? So there are people of all ages throughout eternity. One of the characters turns out to be Homer.

BORGES: Ah yes, of course. In that story there is a man who has lived so long he has forgotten his Homer and lost his Greek. That story is called "The Mortal," I think. But it is written in the baroque style. I don't write that way today. I try to follow the lesson of Kipling's *Plain Tales from the Hills.* Not his later, complex stories but the first stories he wrote. Those are straightforward and they are masterpieces.

CAVETT: You're kind of hard on Carl Sandburg in something I read. You thought he was inferior to—

BORGES: No, I only said he was inferior to Frost, for that stands for eminence. I think that Carl Sandburg was the finest disciple of Walt Whitman. I prefer Carl Sandburg to Edgar Lee Masters. Maybe that's a heresy.

CAVETT: Who do you think is underrated?

BORGES: I think that Emerson, as a poet, is underrated. I think that Emerson was a great poet. Great as a cool, intellectual poet. He seems to be forgotten as a poet. Chesterton also is a great poet, but he seems to be forgotten. Kipling also. When people think about Chesterton, they say, what, he's a Catholic. Kipling is an imperialist. But they are far more than that. They were both men of genius. Oscar Wilde said about Kipling—of course very unjustly and very wittily: "From the point of view of literature, Mr. Kipling is a genius who drops his *h*'s."

CAVETT: Do you ever find it a drawback to be so famous?

BORGES: I feel grateful and at the same time I feel that the whole thing is a huge mistake, that I may be found out at any moment. I will be detected.

CAVETT: You mean discovered.

BORGES: I don't know why I am famous, really. I'm famous, let us say, in spite of the books I've written.

CAVETT: You are very modest, by the way, and self-effacing.

BORGES: I am. I'm really modest. Yes, sir.

CAVETT: There is a story that your translator was trying to translate the phrase "unanimous night."

BORGES: Yes, how priggish, perhaps.

CAVETT: And he said: "What on earth does this mean, 'unanimous night'?"

BORGES: I don't know, really.

CAVETT: Do you feel that it's important to be immortal?

BORGES: I would like to die wholly, body and soul, and be forgotten.

CAVETT: That's your fondest wish.

BORGES: As for my own name, why should I care about it? So awkward a name, Jorge Luis Borges, much like Jorge Luis Jorges or Borge Luis Borges, a tongue twister. I can hardly pronounce it myself.

CAVETT: Well, you've done very well, considering how long you've had to practice.

BORGES: Yes, eighty years. I'm over eighty.

CAVETT: It's been wonderful to meet you and to have you here.

BORGES: It's been wonderful, meeting you, meeting New York, meeting America.

CAVETT: Yes, skyscrapers and all. Thank you, Señor Borges.

BORGES: No, thank you, sir.

4

I Stand Simply
for the Thing I Am

Indiana University,
March 1980

Borges stands for all the things I hate. . . .
I stand simply for the thing I am.

*For this poetry reading, Borges' poems and prose pieces were read in
English by Scott Sanders and Willis Barnstone, and in Spanish by Luis
Beltrán, Miguel Enguídanos, and Jorge Oclander. Following each reading,
Borges commented on his work.*

MY ENTIRE LIFE

Here once again, my lips memory-laden, unique
    and yet similar to you.
I am that torpid intensity which is a soul.
I have persisted in the approach to joy
    and the favoring of pain.
I have crossed the sea.
I have practiced many lands; I have seen a woman
    and two or three men.
I have loved a white and haughty girl
    of Hispanic quietude.
I have seen an infinite suburb where an
    insatiable immortality of sunsets are accomplished.
I have seen some fields where the raw flesh
    of a guitar was painful.
I have savored numerous words.

41

I deeply believe that that is all and that I will
    neither see nor do anything new.
I believe that my days and my nights are equal
    in poverty and richness to those of God and those
    of all men.

                      [Trans. Anthony Kerrigan]

MI VIDA ENTERA

Aquí otra vez, los labios memorables, único y
    semejante a vosotros.
Soy esa torpe intensidad que es un alma.
He persistido en la aproximación de la dicha y
    en la privanza del pesar.
He atravesado el mar.
He conocido muchas tierras; he visto una mujer
    y dos o tres hombres.
He querido a una niña altiva y blanca y de una
    hispánica quietud.
He visto un arrabal infinito donde se cumple una
    insaciada inmortalidad de ponientes.
He paladeado numerosas palabras.
Creo profundamente que eso es todo y que ni veré
    ni ejecutaré cosas nuevas.
Creo que mis jornadas y mis noches se igualan en
    pobreza y en riqueza a las de Dios y a las
    de todos los hombres.

I wrote this poem in a despondent mood. I did not know how many things the future held in store for me. I thought my days were mere repetitions, mere mirrors. But I did not know the gifts that were awaiting me. For example, England, Scotland, Iceland, Sweden, the discovery of America in 1961 in Texas. There I met my friend Enguídanos and also the teaching of English literature. Of course English literature is endless, it cannot be taught. At least I taught my students the love of it or, let us say, the love of the Saxons, of De Quincey, Milton, and so on. And many things were to happen to me—friendship, love, we underwent dictatorship, my mother in prison, my sister in prison, and other things were to come—and they would all lead up to one thing that I never expected: they would all lead up to this evening we are sharing. They would all lead up to Bloomington, Indiana, and to our personal and secret link tonight.

REMORSE

I have committed the worst sin of all
That a man can commit. I have not been
Happy. Let the glaciers of oblivion
Drag me and mercilessly let me fall.
My parents bred and bore me for a higher
Faith in the human game of nights and days;
For earth, for air, for water, and for fire.
I let them down. I wasn't happy. My ways
Have not fulfilled their youthful hope. I gave
My mind to the symmetric stubbornness
Of art, and all its webs of pettiness.
They willed me bravery. I wasn't brave.
It never leaves my side, since I began:
This shadow of having been a brooding man.

[*Trans. Willis Barnstone*]

EL REMORDIMENTO

He cometido el peor de los pecados
Que un hombre puede cometer. No he sido
Feliz. Que los glaciares del olvido
Me arrastren y me pierdan, despiadados.
Mis padres me engendraron para el juego
Arriesgado y hermoso de la vida,
Para la tierra, el agua, el aire, el fuego.
Los defraudé. No fui feliz. Cumplida
No fue su joven voluntad. Mi mente
Se aplicó a las siméntricas porfías
Del arte, que entreteje naderías.

Me legaron valor. No fui valiente.
No me abandona. Siempre está a mi lado
La sombra de haber sido un desdichado.

It comes to me at this moment that Wordsworth wrote that poetry came from emotion recollected in tranquility. That is to say, we undergo happiness or pain. Then we're merely patient. But afterwards, when we recollect it, we are not the actors but the spectators, the onlookers, and *that,* according to Wordsworth, is the best for elicitation of poetry. Now, since I wrote this sonnet some four or five days after my mother's death, when I was still overwhelmed by it, the sonnet cannot be good. But on the other side, many people remember it, many people in Buenos Aires know it by heart, there are discussions of it, they reread it. Personally I think that technically it is worth nothing. But it may be good in some secret way. And now that I have heard it, I like it. Perhaps because Enguídanos read it so well, and perhaps because Willis Barnstone bettered it, improved on it greatly.

THE SEA

Before our human dream (or terror) wove
Mythologies, cosmogonies, and love,
Before time coined its substance into days,
The sea, the always sea, existed: was.
Who is the sea? Who is that violent being,
Violent and ancient, who gnaws the foundations
Of earth? He is both one and many oceans;
He is abyss and splendor, chance and wind.
Who looks on the sea, sees it the first time,
Every time, with the wonder distilled
From elementary things—from beautiful
Evenings, the moon, the leap of a bonfire.
Who is the sea, and who am I? The day
That follows my last agony shall say.

[*Trans. John Updike*]

EL MAR

Antes que el sueño (o el terror) tejiera
Mitologías y cosmogonías,
Antes que el tiempo se acuñara en días,
El mar, el siempre mar, ya estaba y era.
¿Quién es el mar? ¿Quién es aquel violento
Y antiguo ser que roe los pilares
De la tierra y es uno y muchos mares
Y abismo resplandor y azar y viento?
Quien lo mira lo ve por vez primera,
Siempre. Con el asombro que las cosas
Elementales dejan, las hermosas
Tardes, la luna, el fuego de una hoguera.
¿Quién es el mar, quién soy? Lo sabré el día
Ulterior que sucede a la agonía.

I think this poem should be good since the subject is the sea. The sea has been haunting poetry ever since Homer, and in English poetry the sea has been there since earliest times. You find it in the first verses of *Beowulf,* when we are told of the ship of Scyld, the king of Denmark. Then they sent him out to sea in a ship. Then the writer says they sent him to travel far on the power of the sea. And the sea has been always with us. The sea is far more mysterious than the earth. And I don't think you can speak of the sea without the memory of that first chapter of *Moby Dick.* Therein he felt the mystery of the sea. What have I done? I have merely tried to rewrite those ancient poems about the sea. I think back to Camöes of course—*Por mares nunca de antes navegades* "O seas never sailed before"—to *The Odyssey,* to ever so many seas. The sea is haunting us all the time. It is still mysterious to us. We do not know what it is or, as I say in the poem, who he is, since we do not know who we are. That is another mystery. I have written many poems about the sea. This one may perhaps be worth your attention. I don't think I can say anything more, since this poem is not intellectual. That's all to the good. This poem arises from emotion, so it shouldn't be too bad.

G. L. BÜRGER

I can never quite understand
Why I am so bothered by the thing
That happened to Bürger
(his dates are in the encyclopedia),
there, in one of the cities on the plain,
next to the river which has only one bank,
where the palm tree grows, not the pine.
Like all other men,
he told and heard lies,
betrayed and was betrayed,
often agonized over love,
and after sleepless night
saw the gray winter panes of dawn,
but he merited the great voice of Shakespeare
(in which others are heard)
and the voice of Angelus Silesius of Breslau,
and with affected carelessness he polished a line
the way others did in his day.
He knew the present to be nothing
but a fleeting particle of the past
and that we are made of oblivion,
of wisdom useless as Spinoza's corollaries
or the wonders of fear.
In the city by the still river,
about two thousand years after a god's death
(the story I refer to is ancient),
Bürger is alone and now,
precisely now, he is polishing a few lines.

[Trans. Willis Barnstone]

G. L. BÜRGER

No acabo de entender
por qué me afectan de este modo las cosas
que le sucedieron a Bürger
(sus dos fechas están en la enciclopedia)

en una de las ciudades de la llanura,
junto al río que tiene una sola margen
en la que crece la palmera, no el pino.
Al igual de todos los hombres,
dijo y oyó mentiras,
fue traicionado y fue traidor,
agonizó de amor muchas veces
y, tras la noche del insomnio,
vio los cristales grises del alba,
pero mereció la gran voz de Shakespeare
(en la que están las otras)
y la de Angelus Silesius de Breslau
y con falso descuido limó algún verso,
en el estilo de su época.
Sabía que el presente no es otra cosa
que una partícula fugaz del pasado
y que estamos hechos de olvido:
sabiduría tan inútil
como los corolarios de Spinoza
o las magias del miedo.
En la ciudad junto al río inmóvil,
unos dos mil años después de la muerte de un dios
(la historia que refiero es antigua),
Bürger está solo y ahora,
precisamente ahora, lima unos versos.

This poem was given me one afternoon in my apartment in Buenos Aires. I felt very sad and dreary, woebegone, and then I said to myself: Why on earth should I worry what happens to Borges? After all, Borges is nothing, a mere fiction. And then I thought I would write this down. And I bethought myself etymologically—I am always thinking etymology—and I thought: My name, a very common Portuguese name, Borges, means a burger. Then I thought of a German poet, a well-known German poet whose works I suppose I have read. His name is the same as mine, Bürger. Then I thought of a literary trick. I would write a poem about Bürger. And as the reader goes on, he'll find out that Bürger is not Bürger but Borges. After all, we share the same name. Then I began, and I spoke of the city of the plain. That may be the lowlands more than Germany, but also the province of Buenos Aires. And then I gave a hint. I spoke of a palm tree, not the pine, and then I spoke of a river, a river with only one bank to it. And then I remembered the beautiful title of a book by Mallea, *La ciudad junto al río, The City on the River,* and I worked in the line. The reader would find at the end that the poem was not about Bürger but about myself, and that I had played a legitimate trick on him. I hope it works.

BORGES AND I

The other one, the one called Borges, is the one things happen to. I walk through the streets of Buenos Aires and stop for a moment, perhaps mechanically now, to look at the arch of an entrance hall and the grillwork on the gate; I know of Borges from the mail and see his name on a list of professors or in a biographical dictionary. I like hourglasses, maps, eighteenth-century typography, the taste of coffee, and the prose of Stevenson; he shares these preferences, but in a vain way that turns them into the attributes of an actor. It would be an exaggeration to say that ours is a hostile relationship; I live, let myself go on living, so that Borges may contrive his literature, and this literature justifies me. It is no effort for me to confess that he has achieved some valid pages, but those pages cannot save me, perhaps because what is good belongs to no one, not even to him, but rather to the language and to tradition. Besides, I am destined to perish, definitively, and only some instant of myself can survive in him. Little by little, I am giving over everything to him, though I am quite aware of his perverse custom of falsifying and magnifying things. Spinoza knew that all things long to persist in their being; the stone eternally wants to be a stone and the tiger a tiger. I shall remain in Borges, not in myself (if it is true that I am someone), but I recognize myself less in his books than in many others or in the laborious strumming of a guitar. Years ago I tried to free myself from him and went from the mythologies of the suburbs to the games with time and infinity, but those games belong to Borges now and I shall have to imagine other things. Thus my life is a flight and I lose everything and everything belongs to oblivion, or to him.

I do not know which of us has written this page.

[Trans. James E. Irby]

We have just heard the great name, perhaps the forgotten name, of Robert Louis Stevenson. Of course you all remember that he wrote *Jekyll and Hyde,* and from *Jekyll and Hyde* came this page. But in Stevenson's fable the difference between Jekyll and Hyde is that Jekyll is compounded, as all of us, of good and evil while Hyde is compounded of pure evil. And by evil Stevenson did not think of lust, since he did not think of lust as being evil. He thought of cruelty. He thought that cruelty was the forbidden sin, the sin that the Holy Ghost himself would not forgive. Of course the same scheme was used by Oscar Wilde in *The Picture of Dorian Gray,* not so effectively as Stevenson's, but in my case the difference between Borges and I is other. Borges stands for all the things I hate. He stands for publicity, for being photographed, for having interviews, for politics, for opinions—all opinions are despicable I should say. He also stands for those two nonentities, those two imposters failure and success, or, as he called them: where we can meet with triumph and disaster and treat those two imposters just the same. He deals in those things. While *I,* let us say, since the name of the paper is "Borges and I," *I* stands not for the public man but for the private self, for reality, since these other things are unreal to me. The real things are feeling, dreaming, writing—as to publishing, that belongs, I think, to Borges, not to the *I.* Those things should be avoided. Of course I know that the ego has been denied by many philosophers. For example, by David Hume, by Schopenhauer, by Moore, by Macedonio Fernández, by Frances Herbert Bradley. And yet I think we may think of it as a thing. And now it comes to me that I am being helped at this moment by no less a person than William Shakespeare. Remember Sergeant Rolles. Sergeant Rolles was a *miles gloriosus,* a coward. He was degraded. People found out that he wasn't really a brave man. And then Shakespeare came to his aid, and Sergeant Rolles said: "Captain I'll be no longer, simply the thing I am shall make me live, the thing I am." And that of course reminds us of the great words of God: "I am that I am." *Ego sum qui sum.* Well, you may think I stand simply for the thing I am, that intimate and secret thing. Perhaps one day I will find out *who* he is, rather than *what* he is.

ENDYMION ON LATMOS

I was sleeping on the summit and my body
Was beautiful, now worn out by years.
High in the Hellenic night, the centaur
Slowed his fourfold race
To spy into my dream. I liked
To sleep in order to dream and for the other
Lustrous dream eluding memory
That purifies us from the burden
Of being what we are on earth.
Diana, goddess who is also the moon,
Saw me sleeping on the mountain
And slowly came down into my arms
Gold and love in the flaming night.
I held her mortal eyelids,
I wanted to see her lovely face
Which my lips of dust profaned.
I tasted the moon's perfume
And her unending voice called my name.
O pure faces seeking each other,
O rivers of love and of night,
O human kiss and the bow's tension.
How long has my wandering lasted?
There are things unmeasured by grapes
Or flower or slender snow.
People run from me, are threatened
By the man loved by the moon.
Years have gone by. One worry
Horrifies my vigil. I wonder
If that uproar of gold in the mountain
Was true or merely a dream.
Why fool myself that a memory
Of yesterday and a dream are the same?
My loneliness drifts along the ordinary
Roads of the earth, but in the ancient night
Of the Numens, I always seek
The indifferent moon, daughter of Zeus.

[*Trans. Willis Barnstone*]

ENDIMIÓN EN LATMOS

Yo dormía en la cumbre y era hermoso
Mi cuerpo, que los años han gastado.
Alto en la noche helénica, el centauro
Demoraba su cuádruple carrera
Para atisbar mi sueño. Me placía
Dormir para soñar y para el otro
Sueño lustral que elude la memoria
Y que nos purifica del gravamen
De ser aquel que somos en la tierra.
Diana, la diosa que es también la luna,
Me veía dormir en la montaña
Y lentamente descendió a mis brazos
Oro y amor en la encendida noche.
Yo apretaba los párpados mortales,
Yo quería no ver el rostro bello
Que mis labios de polvo profanaban.
Yo aspiré la fragancia de la luna
Y su infinita voz dijo mi nombre.
Oh las puras mejillas que se buscan,
Oh ríos del amor y de la noche,
Oh el beso humano y la tensión del arco.
No sé cuánto duraron mis venturas;
Hay cosas que no miden los racimos
Ni la flor ni la nieve delicada.
La gente me rehuye. Le da miedo
El hombre que fue amado por la luna.
Los años han pasado. Una zozobra
Da horror a mi vigilia. Me pregunto
Si aquel tumulto de oro en la montaña
Fue verdadero o no fue más que un sueño.
Inútil repetirme que el recuerdo
De ayer y un sueño son la misma cosa.
Mi soledad recorre los comunes
Caminos de la tierra, pero siempre
Busco en la antigua noche de los númenes
La indiferente luna, hija de Zeus.

"Endymion on Latmos" is a mythological poem, and perhaps the one personal poem I have ever written. Because Endymion, like all myths, is not a figment or mere reason. Endymion stands for all men. So you say when a man has been loved, then he has been loved by divinity, he has been loved by a goddess, he has been loved by the moon. So I think I have the right to compose this poem, since like all men I have been, at least once or twice, or thrice in my life, Endymion. I have been loved by a goddess. Afterwards I felt unworthy of it, at the same time, grateful. For why should good things last? As Keats had it, "A thing of beauty is a joy forever." The fact of having loved or having been loved, that may be represented by the story of Endymion and the moon, and I have done my best to make this poem alive and not to make you feel that it is based on Lemprière's *Classical Dictionary,* but upon my personal fate and the personal fate of all men, all over the world, all over time.

FRAGMENT

A sword,
An iron sword hammered out in the cold of dawn,
A sword carved with runes
That no one will overlook, that no one will interpret
    in full,
A sword from the Baltic that will be celebrated in
    Northumbria,
A sword that poets
Will equate to ice and fire,
A sword that will be handed from king to king
And from king to dream,
A sword that will be loyal
To an hour known only to Destiny,
A sword that will light up the battle.

A sword to fit the hand
That will guide the beautiful battle, the web of men,
A sword to fit the hand
That will stain with blood the wolf's fangs
And the raven's ruthless beak,

A sword to fit the hand
That will squander red gold,
A sword to fit the hand
That will deal death to the serpent in its golden lair,
A sword to fit the hand
That will gain a kingdom and lose a kingdom,
A sword to fit the hand
That will bring down the forest of spears.
A sword to fit the hand of Beowulf.

[Trans. Norman Thomas di Giovanni]

FRAGMENTO

Una espada,
Una espada de hierro forjada en el frío del alba,
Una espada con runas
Que nadie podrá desoír ni descifrar del todo,
Una espada del Báltico que será cantada en
    Nortumbria,
Una espada que los poetas
Igualarán al hielo y al fuego,
Una espada que un rey dará a otro rey
Y este rey a un sueño,
Una espada que será leal
Hasta una hora que ya sabe el Destino,
Una espada que iluminará la batalla.

Una espada para la mano
Que regirá la hermosa batalla, el tejido de hombres,
Una espada para la mano
Que enrojecerá los dientes del lobo
Y el despiadado pico del cuervo,
Una espada para la mano
Que prodigará el oro rojo,
Una espada para la mano
Que dará muerte a la serpiente en su lecho de oro,
Una espada para la mano
Que ganará un reino y perderá un reino,
Una espada para la mano

Que derribará la selva de lanzas.
Una espada para la mano de Beowulf.

This poem should be my best one since Rudyard Kipling wrote it and called it "The Thing." But the occasion was different. I was staying a few months in Texas, in Austin, a city I greatly loved, and there I read, or reread, *Historia del modernismo, History of Modernism,* by Federico Riña, and therein I found a beautiful sonnet by a Bolivian poet. I will not try to translate, since it is untranslatable. I think I can recover the first stanza, and it runs thus—you should try to hear the lilt in Spanish:

Peregrina paloma imaginaria
que enardeces los últimos amores,
alma de luz, de música y de flor,
peregrina paloma imaginaria.

(Imaginary pilgrim dove
who gives fire to the final loves,
soul of light, of music and of flower,
pilgrim soul imagined.)

Then I said to myself: This poem means absolutely nothing and it's very beautiful. That thing happens. For example, to fall back on Shakespeare, when we read "Music to hear for here is how music saddens/ sweets with sweets warmed, joy delights in joy." When we read those line that recall Verlaine, that prophesy Verlaine, we do not think of the meaning. We think of the sound and symbols and that's that. Then I said I will attempt the same thing. I will write a beautiful poem—I wonder if I have succeeded—and, in order to succeed, a meaningless poem. I fell back on one of my passions, the passions of things Old English and Old Norse, and I recollected the kennings used by the Saxons and by the Norsemen. Then I wrote that poem rather in the manner of a nursery rhyme that begins "This is the house that Jack built," and then you go on to other things. Well, I began merely by speaking of the sword, and then of the hand that wielded it, and then of the Nordics, and so on. And in the end I gave the solution. The solution was less important than the poem itself, less important than the sounds, the symbols, the presence of things Northern and ancient. In the end I said: *Una espada para la mano de Beowulf* "A sword to fit the hand of Beowulf." I attempted this experiment, the one experiment I tried of writing beautiful and meaningless poetry. I hope I succeeded.

THE MOON

for María Kodama

There is such loneliness in that gold.
The moon of the nights is not the moon
Which the first Adam saw. The long centuries
Of human vigil have filled her
With ancient lament. Look at her. She is your mirror.

[*Trans. Willis Barnstone*]

LA LUNA

a María Kodama

Hay tanta soledad en ese oro.
La luna de las noches no es la luna
Que vio el primer Adán. Los largos siglos
De la vigilia humana la han colmado
De antiguo llanto. Mírala. Es tu espejo.

Perhaps we are allowed to ask a few words. I think that poetry, that memory, that oblivion have enriched the word. I wonder if the word *moon,* that lingering English word, is precisely the same as the Latin or Spanish *luna.* I suppose they are slightly different, and that slight difference may be all important, for all we know. But in this case I thought of generations of men looking long and long at the moon and thinking of it and changing it into myths, for example, the myth of Endymion on Latmos. And then I thought to myself: When I look at the moon I'm not looking simply at a luminous volume in the sky. I'm also looking at the moon of Virgil, of Shakespeare, of Verlaine, of Góngora. And so I wrote that poem. I think the first line should not be forgotten—*Hay tanta soledad en ese oro* "There is such loneliness in that gold"—since without it the poem might fall to pieces—perhaps it has. For after all, writing poetry is a very mysterious thing. The poet should not tamper with what he writes, he should not intrude himself into his writing. Let the writing do itself. Let the Holy Ghost or the muse or the subconscious —to give it an ugly contemporary name—have its way and then perhaps we make up poetry. Even I may write a poem.

A YELLOW ROSE

The illustrious Giambattista Marino, whom the unanimous mouths of Fame—to use an image dear to him—proclaimed the new Homer and the new Dante, did not die that afternoon or the next. And yet, the immutable and tacit event that happened then was in effect the last event of his life. Laden with years and glory, the man lay dying in a vast Spanish bed with carved bedposts. It takes no effort to imagine a lordly balcony, facing west, a few steps away, and, further down, the sight of marble and laurels and a garden whose stone steps are duplicated in a rectangle of water. A woman has placed a yellow rose in a vase. The man murmurs the inevitable verses which—to tell the truth—have begun to weary him a little:

> Blood of the garden, pomp of the walk,
> gem of spring, April's eye. . . .

Then came the revelation. Marino *saw* the rose as Adam might have seen it in Paradise. And he sensed that it existed in its eternity and not in his words, and that we may make mention or allusion of a thing but never express it at all; and that the tall proud tomes that cast a golden penumbra in an angle of the drawing room were not—as he had dreamed in his vanity—a mirror of the world, but simply one more thing added to the universe.

This illumination came to Marino on the eve of his death, and, perhaps, it had come to Homer and Dante too.

[Trans. Anthony Kerrigan]

THE OTHER TIGER

I think of a tiger. Half-light exalts
The vast busy library
And seems to set the bookshelves back;
Strong, innocent, bloodstained, fresh,
It wanders through the jungle and its morning
And prints its tracks on the muddy
Banks of a river whose name it doesn't know
(In its world there are no names or past
Or future, only a definite now)
And slips through barbaric distances,
Sniffing smells in the braided labyrinths

Out of the smell of deer;
Among the stripes of the bamboo tree
I decipher the tiger's stripes and feel
Its bony frame under the splendid quivering hide.
The curving seas and deserts of the planet
Futilely intervene;
From this house in a remote port
In South America I track you and dream you,
O tiger of the Ganges' banks.

As evening fills my soul I think
The tiger addressed in my poem
Is a tiger of symbols and shadows,
A string of literary tropes
And scraps from the encyclopedia
And not the fatal tiger, the deadly jewel
That under the sun or changing moon
Goes on in Sumatra or Bengal fulfilling
Its round of love, indolence and death.
To the tiger of symbols I oppose
The real one, with hot blood,
Decimating a herd of buffaloes
And today, August 3rd, 1959,
A deliberate shadow spreads over the grass
But already in the act of naming it
And conjecturing its world
It becomes a fiction, art, and not a living beast
Among beasts roaming the earth.

We will seek a third tiger. Like
The others it will be a shape
From my dream, a system of words,
And not the vertebrate tiger
That, beyond all mythologies,
Paces the earth. I know all this
Yet something drives me to this vague,
Insane and ancient adventure, and I go on,
Searching through hours of the afternoon
For the other tiger, not in the poem.

[*Trans. Willis Barnstone*]

EL OTRO TIGRE

And the craft that createth a semblance
—Morris, *Sigurd the Volsung* (*1876*)

Pienso en un tigre. La penumbra exalta
La vasta Biblioteca laboriosa
Y parece alejar los anaqueles;
Fuerte, inocente, ensangrentado y nuevo,
El irá por su selva y su mañana
Y marcará su rastro en la limosa
Margen de un río cuyo nombre ignora
(En su mundo no hay nombres ni pasado
Ni porvenir, sólo un instante cierto)
Y salvará las bárbaras distancias
Y husmeará en el trenzado laberinto
De los olores el olor del alba
Y el olor deleitable del venado;
Entre las rayas del bambú descifro
Sus rayas y presiento la osatura
Bajo la piel espléndida que vibra.
En vano se interponen los convexos
Mares y los desiertos del planeta;
Desde esta casa de un remoto puerto
De América del Sur, te sigo y sueño,
Oh tigre de las márgenes del Ganges.

Cunde la tarde en mi alma y reflexiono
Que el tigre vocativo de mi verso
Es un tigre de símbolos y sombras,
Una serie de tropos literarios
Y de memorias de la enciclopedia
Y no el tigre fatal, la aciaga joya
Que, bajo el sol o la diversa luna,
Va cumpliendo en Sumatra o en Bengala
Su rutina de amor, de ocio y de muerte.
Al tigre de los símbolos he opuesto
El verdadero, el de caliente sangre,
El que diezma la tribu de los búfalos
Y hoy, 3 de agosto del 59,

Alarga en la pradera una pausada
Sombra, pero ya el hecho de nombrarlo
Y de conjeturar su circunstancia
Lo hace ficción del arte y no criatura
Viviente de las que andan por la tierra.

Un tercer tigre buscaremos. Este
Será como los otros una forma
De mi sueño, un sistema de palabras
Humanas y no el tigre vertebrado
Que, más allá de las mitologías,
Pisa la tierra. Bien lo sé, pero algo
Me impone esta aventura indefinida,
Insensata y antigua, y persevero
En buscar por el tiempo de la tarde
El otro tigre, el que no está en el verso.

Both poems, "The Yellow Rose" and "The Other Tiger," are of course the same, using different symbols. I wrote the "Yellow Rose." Years afterwards I thought that the yellow rose was of no avail, and I attempted it once more, with another symbol, not the rose but a tiger. Then I wrote "The Other Tiger." Of course in the second poem we are not to think of three tigers. We have to think of an unending chain of tigers. They are all linked and they are all force. That is to say, this poem has, I am sorry to say, a moral. This poem stands for the fact that things are unobtainable by art. At the same time, though things may be unobtainable, though we shall never find the yellow rose or the other tiger, we are making structures of words, of symbols, of metaphors, of adjectives, of images, and those things exist, and that world is not the world of the rose and the tiger but the world of art, which may be as praiseworthy and as real. For all I know, these poems that came out of despair, out of feeling that art is hopeless, that you cannot express things and that you can only allude to them—these poems may also be hope and a token of felicity, since if we cannot ape nature we can still make art. And that might be sufficient for man, for any man, for a lifetime.

THE CAUSES

The sunsets and the generations.
The days and none was the first.
The freshness of water in Adam's
Throat. Orderly Paradise.
The eye disciphering the darkness.
The love of wolves at dawn.
The word. The hexameter. The mirror.
The Tower of Babel and pride.
The moon which the Chaldeans gazed at.
The uncountable sands of the Ganges.
Chuang-Tzu and the butterfly that dreams him.
The golden apples on the islands.
The steps in the wandering labyrinth.
Penelope's infinite tapestry.
The circular time of the Stoics.
The coin in the mouth of the dead man.
The sword's weight on the scale.
Each drop of water in the water-clock.
The eagles, the memorable days, the legions.
Caesar on the morning of Pharsalis.
The shadow of crosses over the earth.
The chess and algebra of the Persians.
The footprints of long migration.
The sword's conquest of kingdoms.
The relentless compass. The open sea.
The clock echoing in the memory.
The king executed by the axe.
The incalculable dust that was armies.
The voice of the nightingale in Denmark.
The calligrapher's meticulous line.
The suicide's face in the mirror.
The gambler's card. Greedy gold.
The forms of a cloud in the desert.
Every arabesque in the kaleidoscope.
Each regret and each tear.
All those things were made perfectly clear.
So our hands could meet.

[*Trans. Willis Barnstone*]

LAS CAUSAS

Los ponientes y las generaciones.
Los días y ninguno fue el primero.
La frescura del agua en la garganta
De Adán. El ordenado Paraíso.
El ojo descifrando la tiniebla.
El amor de los lobos en el alba.
La palabra. El hexámetro. El espejo.
La Torre de Babel y la soberbia.
La luna que miraban los caldeos.
Las arenas innúmeras del Ganges.
Chuang-Tzu y la mariposa que lo sueña.
Las manzanas de oro de las islas.
Los pasos del errante laberinto.
El infinito lienzo de Penélope.
El tiempo circular de los estoicos.
La moneda en la boca del que ha muerto.
El peso de la espada en la balanza.
Cada gota de agua en la clepsidra.
Las águilas, los fastos, las legiones.
César en la mañana de Farsalia.
La sombra de las cruces en la tierra.
El ajedrez y el álgebra del persa.
Los rastros de las largas migraciones.
La conquista de reinos por la espada.
La brújula incesante. El mar abierto.
El eco del reloj en la memoria.
El rey ajusticiado por el hacha.
El polvo incalculable que fue ejércitos.
La voz del ruiseñor en Dinamarca.
La escrupulosa línea del calígrafo.
El rostro del suicida en el espejo.
El naipe del tahúr. El oro ávido.
Las formas de la nube en el desierto.
Cada arabesco del calidoscopio.
Cada remordimiento y cada lágrima.
Se precisaron todas esas cosas
Para que nuestras manos se encontraran.

Our hands had met at long last, and I was aware that, in order for that felicitous thing to happen, the whole of the past was needed. When something happens, it has been formed by the profound, by the unfathomable, past, by the chain of causes and effects and of course there is no first cause. Every cause is the effect of another. All things branch out into infinity. This may be an abstract idea. At the same time I felt it to be true. And I think that this poem is a true poem in the sense that, though it includes many tropes and metaphors, the strength of the poem does not lie in each line or metaphor or in adjectives or in rhetorical tricks but in the fact that what the poem says is true: that all the past, all the unfathomable past, has been made in order to arrive at the particular moment. Then the past is justified. If there is a moment of happiness, of human happiness, then that is due to many terrible things that have come before, but also to the many beautiful things. The past is making us, making us all the time. I think of the past not as something awful but as a kind of fountain. And all things come from that fountain. That was the feeling I had, the awareness I had, and I did my best to deal with it. And speaking of the past, I refer not only to things that have historically happened—since history is frivolous and irrelevant—but to myths. Myths are far more important. And so I began with myth. I spoke of Hamlet, I spoke of Greek mythology, of things that have happened not in history but in the dreams of men. So I think this poem may be justified.

CONJECTURAL POEM

> *Doctor Francisco Laprida, assassinated September 22, 1829, by the irregulars of Aldao, reflects before he dies:*

The bullets whine on the last afternoon.
The wind is up, and full of ashes,
dispersing the day and the formless
war, and victory belongs to them,
to the barbarians: the gauchos have won.
And Francisco Narciso de Laprida, I,

who studied canon law and civil,
whose voice declared the independence
of these harsh provinces, am overthrown,
covered with blood and sweat,
without fear or hope, lost,
fleeing south through the farthest outskirts.
I'm like that captain in *Purgatorio*
fleeing afoot and leaving a trail of blood,
blinded and felled by death
where a dark river loses its name:
that's the way I'll fall. Today's the end.
The lateral night of the plains
lies in ambush to waylay me. I hear the hoofs
of my own hot death, searching me out,
I longed to be something else, a man of
sentiments, books, judgment,
and now will lie in a swamp under the open sky.
And yet, a secret joy inexplicably
exalts me. I've met my destiny,
my final South American destiny.
The manifold labyrinth my steps
wove through all these years since childhood
has brought me to this ruinous afternoon.
Now at this last point I find
the recondite code and cipher to my days,
the fate of Francisco de Laprida,
the missing letter, the perfect
form known to God from the start.
In the mirror of this night I find
the unexpected mien of my eternity.
The circle's closing. Thus may it be.
My feet are treading the shadows of pikes
pointed at me. The taunts of death,
the riders, the horses and their manes
are circling around me, hovering, the first
blow of the hard iron to rip at my chest,
the intimate knife at my throat . . .

[*Trans. Anthony Kerrigan*]

POEMA CONJETURAL

*El doctor Francisco Laprida, asesinado
el día 22 de setiembre de 1829 por los
montoneros de Aldao, piensa antes de
morir:*

Zumban las balas en la tarde última.
Hay viento y hay cenizas en el viento,
se dispersan el día y la batalla
deforme, y la victoria es de los otros.
Vencen los bárbaros, los gauchos vencen.
Yo, que estudié las leyes y los cánones,
yo, Francisco Narciso de Laprida,
cuya voz declaró la independencia
de estas crueles provincias, derrotado,
de sangre y de sudor manchado el rostro,
sin esperanza ni temor, perdido,
huyo hacia el Sur por arrabales últimos.

Como aquel capitán del Purgatorio
que, huyendo a pie y ensangrentando el llano,
fue cegado y tumbado por la muerte
donde un oscuro río pierde el nombre,
así habré de caer. Hoy es el término.
La noche lateral de los pantanos
me acecha y me demora. Oigo los cascos
de mi caliente muerte que me busca
con jinetes, con belfos y con lanzas.

Yo que anhelé ser otro, ser un hombre
de sentencias, de libros, de dictámenes,
a cielo abierto yaceré entre ciénagas;
pero me endiosa el pecho inexplicable
un júbilo secreto. Al fin me encuentro
con mi destino sudamericano.
A esta ruinosa tarde me llevaba
el laberinto múltiple de pasos
que mis días tejieron desde un día
de la niñez. Al fin he descubierto
la recóndita clave de mis años,

la suerte de Francisco de Laprida,
la letra que faltaba, la perfecta
forma que supo Dios desde el principio.
En el espejo de esta noche alcanzo
mi insospechado rostro eterno. El círculo
se va a cerrar. Yo aguardo que así sea.

Pisan mis pies la sombra de las lanzas
que me buscan. Las befas de mi muerte,
los jinetes, las crines, los caballos,
se ciernen sobre mí. . . . Ya el primer golpe,
ya el duro hierro que me raja el pecho,
el íntimo cuchillo en la garganta.

The scheme of this poem is by Browning. In Browning we read the romantic monologues and there we can follow the feelings of a man. And then I thought: I will do my best, a Stevenson habit, I will play the sedulous ape to Browning and attempt a poem. But it might be striking if what the hero of the poem is thinking should be made to form his last moments, and then I bethought myself of Francisco Narciso de Laprida, the president of the first revolutionary congress in 1816, a kinsman, who was killed by the gauchos. Then I said to myself: I will try to recover not those things but to imagine what he may have thought when he was defeated by barbarians. He was the man who wanted our country to be a civilized country. He was defeated, pursued by barbarians. He had his throat cut. Then I remembered Dante's *Purgatorio,* and the line came to me: *Fuggendo a piede e sanguinado il piano.** My Italian is weak but I think that is the right line. I wove that into my poem: [*que,*] *huyendo a pie y ensangrentando el llano* "[who] fleeing on foot left blood on the plain." And I published this poem—it was rejected, I'm sorry to say, by a newspaper whose name I have no cause to mention—but it was published in the periodical *Sur.* This poem is not only an historical poem but, when I wrote it, I was writing what we all felt, because the dictatorship had come, and we complained of being Paris or being Madrid or Rome. But really we were South Americans and there was the dictator. So the poet says: *Al fin me encuentro con mi destino sudamericano* "I see at last that I am face to face with my South

Purgatorio, Canto V, l. 99.

American destiny." So I wrote the poem. The poem goes on. The horseman finds the man who is being hunted down by them, and the poem ends with the death of the man. We have the last verse and the last verse is the last moment of his life, when his throat is cut. Thus when I write *el íntimo cuchillo en la gárganta* "across my throat the intimate knife," this is the last verse that may be written, since after that he may be annihilated. He may find his way into another world, we do not know, but the poem, I think, has a certain tragic strength to it since it ends when the man dies. The poem ends with the last verse. They go together.

A BOOK

Scarcely a thing among things
But also a weapon. It was forged
In England, in 1604,
And they weighted it with a dream. It holds
Sound and fury and night and scarlet.
My palm feels its heaviness. Who could say
It contains hell: the bearded
Witches who are fates, the daggars
Which carry out laws of shadow,
The delicate castle air
That will see you die, the delicate
Hand capable of bloodying the seas,
The sword and shouting of the battle.

That silent uproar sleeps
In the circle of one of the books
On the quiet shelf. It sleeps and waits.

[*Trans. Willis Barnstone*]

UN LIBRO

Apenas una cosa entre las cosas
Pero también un arma. Fue forjada
En Inglaterra, en 1604,

Y la cargaron con un sueño. Encierra
Sonido y furia y noche y escarlata.
Mi palma la sopesa. Quién diría
Que contiene el infierno: las barbadas
Brujas que son las parcas, los puñales
Que ejecutan las leyes de la sombra,
El aire delicado del castillo
Que te verá morir, la delicada
Mano capaz de ensangrentar los mares,
La espada y el clamor de la batalla.

Ese tumulto silencioso duerme
En el ámbito de uno de los libros
Del tranquilo anaquel. Duerme y espera.

We think of all books, not only holy writ but the others, as being holy. And that is right, since our tools, our tools framed by mankind, are mere extensions of his hand—a sword, a plow. And a telescope or a microscope is an extension of his eyesight. But in the case of books, there is far more than that. A book is an extension of the imagination, of memory. Books are perhaps the only thing we know of the past, of our personal past also. And yet, what is a book? A book, when it lies in the bookshelf—I think Emerson has said so (I like to be indebted to Emerson, one of my heroes)—a book is a thing among things. And after all, why should it be revealed? A book is a thing and there it is. It has no existence of its own. A book is unaware of itself until the reader comes. And then I bethought myself of writing a poem about that very simple fact: that a book is a physical object in a world of physical objects. Since I had to choose a certain book, I thought of *Macbeth*. Were I to choose a single tragedy of Shakespeare, I think I would choose *Macbeth,* that tense thing that begins: "When shall we three meet again/ in thunder, lightning or in rain?" And then goes on: "Life is a tale told by an idiot, full of sound and fury, signifying nothing." Another character who speaks "of this dead butcher and his fiendish greed." Of course Macbeth was far more than a "dead butcher." Then I thought, well, here is a volume. We find that in this volume the tragedy of Macbeth is enclosed, all the din, the uproar, the weird sisters. *Weird* is not an adjective in this case. *Weird* is a noun since it stands for the Saxon *wurd* "fate." The witches are also fate, the weird sisters. And this book is dead, this book is lifeless, and this book in a sense is lurking, is awaiting us. So I wrote the last line. I think it runs: "It sleeps and waits."

5

A Crowd Is
an Illusion

Columbia University,
March 1980

A crowd is an illusion. . . . I am talking to
you personally.

WILLIS BARNSTONE: Borges, in every literature authors use myth.
Joyce, Milton, Virgil did so. Your own work has many myths in it. Could
you tell us about the use of myth in your own writing?

JORGE LUIS BORGES: I have never attempted myth. Myth was *given*
me, perhaps, by the readers, but I never attempted it or thought about it.

BARNSTONE: Why did you choose to write a poem about Endymion?

BORGES: I wrote a poem of Endymion because I wanted to say that
Endymion is a matter of fact and not myth, since every man who has
been loved has been loved by a goddess. I have been Endymion. All of
us have been Endymion who have been loved by the moon, who have felt
unworthy of it, and who have sought to thank it. That was the meaning
of the poem. I wasn't playing around with myth.

BARNSTONE: You have done a lot of translation in your day. When
you translate from other languages, do you feel that you've learned
something for your own poetry?

BORGES: Yes, not only when I translate but when I read. I'm learning
all the time. I'm a disciple, not a master.

BARNSTONE: To what extent do you think that books in translation
have changed the Spanish language or the English language? That is,
does the existence of, say, the King James translation in English affect
the use of the English language?

BORGES: I think the King James translation of the Bible is really the
book of England. I think of it as being the essential book, even as Wordsworth is essential, even as Chaucer is essential. I don't think of Shake-

69

speare as being essential—I think of him as being alien to the English tradition, since the English go in for understatement and Shakespeare goes in for violent metaphors. So when I think of an English writer, I tend to think of Johnson, of Wordsworth, of Coleridge, of course. And why not of Robert Frost? He was an English writer also!

BARNSTONE: I wanted to ask you about your use in your own poems of free verse and also of traditional forms such as the sonnet.

BORGES: I think that free verse is the most difficult of all forms of verse, unless you take the precaution of being Walt Whitman! I think that the classic forms are easier because they provide you with a pattern. Now, I'm merely repeating what Stevenson said. Stevenson wrote that when you had a verse, a unit, then you would go on repeating that unit. That unit might be made by alliteration (as in the case of Old English poems and Old Norse poems), or by rhyme, or by a certain number of syllables, or by short or long accents. But once you have a unit, you merely have to repeat the pattern. In the case of prose, the pattern has to be changed all the time. It should be changed in a way pleasing to the reader, pleasing to the ear. And that may be the reason why verse, in all literatures, comes before prose. Verse is easier, especially if there is a form to be followed.

Now in the case of free verse, free verse is as difficult as prose, I should say. Many people think that when we speak orally we use prose. It's a misconception. I think that oral language is alien to literature. I think of prose as being very difficult. Prose should always come after classic verse. Of course I made the mistake that all young men do, to think that free verse was easier. So my first book was a failure in many senses: not only in that no copies were sold (I never intended that!), but in the sense that the verses were very awkward. I should advise the young poet to begin by the classic forms and patterns.

One of the most beautiful of all patterns, I should say, is the sonnet. What a strange thing that a form that seems so haphazard as the sonnet —two stanzas, two quartets, or three stanzas, then two rhyming lines— should be used for such different purposes! If I think of a sonnet by Shakespeare, a sonnet by Milton, a sonnet by Rossetti, a sonnet by Swinburne, a sonnet by William Butler Yeats, I am thinking of things that are entirely different. Yet the structure is the same, for that structure allows the voice to find its own intonation, so that sonnets all over the world have the same structure and are entirely different. Each poet contributes something to it. So I would advise a young poet to begin by rigorous stanzas.

BARNSTONE: Would you like to compare the various sonnets in the English language with the use of sonnets in the Spanish language and your own writing of sonnets?

BORGES: My own writing of sonnets should be forgotten. We speak of literature!

BARNSTONE: Nevertheless, your own writing of sonnets has something to do with the English language.

BORGES: Well, I hope it has. Of course the Spanish sonnets can be very different also. If we take a sonnet by Góngora, a sonnet by Garcilaso, a sonnet by Quevedo, by Lugones, by Enrique Banchs, they are quite different. And yet the form is the same. But the voice, the intonation behind the sonnet, is completely distinct.

BARNSTONE: Borges, if I could return to another kind of question, a personal question, and ask you about your feelings: When have you had a feeling of peace, if ever?

BORGES: Yes, but perhaps not now. Yes, I have had some moments of peace. They were given me perhaps sometimes by mere solitude. Sometimes by books, and sometimes in memory. And sometimes when I wake and find myself strangely enough in Japan or in New York. Those are very pleasant gifts and moments of peace.

BARNSTONE: When have you felt moments of fear?

BORGES: I am feeling it now at this moment. I have stage fright.

BARNSTONE: Any other moments?

BORGES: Well, I have felt also the fear of beauty. Sometimes reading Swinburne, or reading Rossetti, or reading Yeats, or reading Wordsworth, I may have thought, well, this is too beautiful. I am unworthy of the verses I am reading. But I have felt fear also. Before writing I always think: Who am I to attempt writing? What do I know about it? And then I make a fool of myself—but I've done that so many times one more time won't matter. And I also fear that certain fear before the blank page. And then I say to myself: After all, what does it matter? I've written far too many books. What else can I do but go on writing, since literature seems to be—I will not say "my destiny"—my "to do," and I am grateful for it. The only kind of destiny I can imagine.

BARNSTONE: Recently you spoke about having experienced, twice, moments you would call timeless, mystical. Would you be willing to speak about the unspeakable?

BORGES: Yes. Two timeless moments have been given me. One came through quite an ordinary way. Suddenly I felt somehow I am beyond time. And the other came after a woman had told me that she couldn't love me and I felt very unhappy. I went for a long walk. I went to a railway station in the south of Buenos Aires. Then, suddenly, I got that feeling of timelessness, of eternity. I don't know how long it lasted, since it was timeless. But I felt very grateful for it. Then I wrote a poem on the railway station wall (I shouldn't have done that!). The poem is still there. So I've had the experience only twice in my life. But at the same time, I know people who've never had it and I know people who are having it all the time. My friend, a mystic, for example, abounds in ecstacies. I don't. I've only had two experiences of timeless time in eighty years.

BARNSTONE: When you are in time—

BORGES: I'm in time all the time.

BARNSTONE: The other ninety-eight moments of your life, there's the time of your mind, of dream, and then there's the external time, the clock time, the measured time. You talk and write very much about time.

BORGES: Time is the essential riddle.

BARNSTONE: Would you speak to us about the time of dream?

BORGES: If you use the word *dream,* I think of it in terms of that tiger of the dream, the nightmare. I have the nightmare every other night. The pattern is always the same. I find myself, let's say, always on a street corner in Buenos Aires, or in a room, quite an ordinary room, and then I attempt another street corner and another room and they are the same. That goes on and on. Then I say to myself, well, this is the nightmare of the labyrinth. I merely have to wait, and I wake up in due time. But sometimes I dream I wake up and find myself on the same street corner, in the same room, or in the same marshland, ringed in by the same fog or looking into the same mirror—and then I know that I am not really awake. I go on dreaming until I wake, but the nightmare feeling lasts for two minutes, perhaps, until I feel that I am going mad. Then suddenly all that vanishes. I can go back to sleep. One of my bad habits, the nightmare, I should say.

BARNSTONE: One of your old habits is friendship.

BORGES: All of my habits are old.

BARNSTONE: What has happened to your friendships over the last sixty years?

BORGES: Unhappily, when I think of my friends, I am thinking of dead men or dead ladies. But I have still some living friends. Of course at my age I have practically no contemporaries. Who is to blame? Nobody. I should have died long before. And yet still, life has made for good, since I am here in America and since I am among you.

BARNSTONE: You have contempt for most fame and even for your own publications.

BORGES: Of course.

BARNSTONE: Yet today we're speaking to this very friendly group here. Tell me how you feel about speaking to them and letting them in on your knowledge.

BORGES: I am not speaking to them. I am speaking to every individual of you. After all, a crowd is an illusion. No such thing exists. I am talking to you personally. Walt Whitman had it: "Is it right, are we here together alone?" Well, we are alone, you and I, and *you* stands for an individual, not for the crowd, which is nonexistent, of course. Even I myself may be nonexistent also.

AUDIENCE: It is said that you are very fond of New York City.

BORGES: I am of course. I am not a lunatic!

AUDIENCE: Why do you think New York City is such a special place?

BORGES: I will tell you of what Adolfo Bioy Casares told me. He said: "I love Buenos Aires" (that's his hometown and my hometown), "I love London, I love Rome, I love Paris, but when I came to New York, I thought I'd spent all my life in the provinces. Here's the capital city." He felt very happy about it and so do I. Here we are in the capital.

AUDIENCE: We're in a library now. What about your story "The Library"?

BORGES: Yes, I wrote that story when I was playing the sedulous ape to Kafka. I wrote it forty years ago and I don't remember it, really.

AUDIENCE: You once said that a writer starts out to describe a kingdom of castles and horses, but ends by tracing the lines of his own face.

BORGES: Did I say that? I wish I had said that! Ah, but of course, I remember that page. It is about a man who has an endless world before him and then he begins drawing of ships, of anchors, of towers, of horses, of birds, and so on. In the end he finds out that what he has designed is a picture of his own face. That, of course, is a metaphor of the writer: what the writer leaves behind him is not what he has written, but his image. So that is added to the written word. In the case of many writers, every page may be poor, but the sum total is the image the writer leaves of himself. The image, for example, of Edgar Allan Poe is far superior, I should say, to any one of the pages Poe wrote (even that very wonderful *Narrative of Arthur Gordon Pym,* his best work). So that may be the destiny of a writer.

AUDIENCE: Would you talk about your interest in Judaism?

BORGES: I suppose there are many reasons. Firstly, my grandmother was English, from a stock of preachers. So I was brought up, let's say, hearing the English Bible over and over again. And then, I have done my best to be a Jew. I may have failed. And there are some names in my family which are Jewish: Acevedo and Pinedo. And what is more important, if we belong to Western civilization then all of us, despite the many adventures of the blood, all of us are Greeks and Jews. And if we are Christians, then of course we also belong to the Bible and to the Jews.

I owe so many things to the Jews. I taught myself German way back in 1917, and I found the very best method of doing so: I got a copy of Heinrich Heine's poetry and a German-English dictionary. For people who are learning English, I always tell them to begin by reading Oscar Wilde, though Wilde was a minor poet, and Heine, of course, was a man of genius, as we all know. I have also dabbled in the Kabbalah, I wrote a poem on the Golem, and I have written many poems on Israel. But I wonder if those reasons are sufficient. I suppose they are. Many a time I think of myself as a Jew, but I wonder whether I have the right to think so. It may be wishful thinking.

AUDIENCE: Do you have any plans to write part three of *Don Quixote?*

BORGES: No. Nothing is to be expected or feared from me.

AUDIENCE: In your writing, you concern yourself with the uncanny, the supernatural, the fantastic. Why is this?

BORGES: You might as well ask "Why am I interested in love or in the moon?" I don't see anything strange about it. Of course the word *uncanny* exists only in the Germanic languages. In Romance languages, people did not feel the need for that word. But I do, partly because of my English blood, perhaps. I have a feeling for the uncanny. Many people don't, since there is no such word in Spanish. There is a fine Scottish word, *eerie,* that also stands for something not felt by Latin people.

AUDIENCE: What is the difference between your impulse in writing poetry and in writing prose?

BORGES: Poetry and prose are essentially the same thing. There is only formal difference. But there is also a difference in the reader. For example, if you look at a printed page in prose, then you expect or fear information or advice or arguments, while if you see something printed as verse, then you feel that what you will take in is emotion, passion, sadness, felicity, or whatever it may be. But essentially I suppose they are the same.

AUDIENCE: In "Pierre Menard" [*Ficciones*], you discuss the literary technique of creative anachronism. What literary anachronisms do you see today?

BORGES: I wonder if anachronism is possible. Since we're all living in the same century, we are all writing the same book and thinking the same things. For example, Flaubert sat down to write a novel about Carthage, but if I had to name a typical nineteenth-century French novel I would choose *Salambô*. It could not have been otherwise. And even such a fine piece as *Caesar and Cleopatra* by George Bernard Shaw, you can see that it was not written in Rome or in Israel. It was written in the twentieth century by an Irishman. You can detect those things. I don't think anachronism is possible. Unhappily for us, we belong to a certain time, we belong to certain habits. We are using contemporary language, and that's that.

AUDIENCE: Please discuss the character of "Funes the Memorious."

BORGES: I wrote that story as a metaphor, or allegory, of insomnia. Because I had been sleepless many nights over, and then I thought that a man bordering on infinite memory would go mad. I was suffering under insomnia at the time, and oddly enough, after writing that story I began to sleep quite well. I hope the story hasn't sent you to sleep.

BARNSTONE: Of all the characters you've created—if you've created any—

BORGES: No, I haven't. It was always the same old Borges, only slightly disguised.

BARNSTONE: —who is the one you feel closest to?

BORGES: I wonder if I have created any characters. I don't think so. I am always writing about myself, using different myths.

BARNSTONE: Does Funes have a priority among those characters whom you've not created?

BORGES: Yes. I think of that story as being quite a good story though I wrote it.

AUDIENCE: Why, among your stories, are there characters who appear to be intellectually pretentious?

BORGES: I suppose because *I* am pretentious. I am a bit of a prig.

BARNSTONE: You're asked to say something about "Death and the Compass."

BORGES: I hardly remember that story. It was meant to be a detective story. It won a second prize in an Ellery Queen mystery magazine—I'm very proud of it.

AUDIENCE: Have you ever suffered from writer's block?

BORGES: What is that?

BARNSTONE: When you can't write because your mind runs dry.

BORGES: It runs dry all the time but I pretend it doesn't.

AUDIENCE: What do you think about Julio Cortázar?

BORGES: I remember Cortázar. Some thirty years ago I was editing a small and almost secret magazine* and he came to me with a story and wanted to have my opinion on it. I said: "Come back within ten days." He came back before the week was out. And I told him the story was being printed and my sister was doing illustrations for it. That story was a very fine story, and the only thing I've read by him, called "La casa tomada," "The House Taken Over." I saw him no more. We met once in Paris and he reminded me of the episode—and that's that. You see, I am old, blind, I do not read my contemporaries. But I do remember that very fine story and the illustrations made by my sister. And that was the first time he got something printed in Buenos Aires. I was his first publisher.

AUDIENCE: What memories do you have about Macedonio Fernández?

BORGES: I am remembering him all the time. Macedonio Fernández was a man of genius—not always in his writings but always in his almost silent conversation. You could not speak to Macedonio without being intelligent. I remember a cousin of mine, who is dead now. Macedonio once asked him were there many people at a concert, and he answered that there were so few that people were left out in droves. Macedonio liked that joke and my cousin gave it to him. I asked my cousin why on earth he gave that joke to Macedonio. And he said because if it were not

The Annals of Buenos Aires.

for Macedonio he would not have made that joke. Macedonio obliged all of us, even me, to be intelligent, and that by his silence. He spoke in a very low voice, but he was thinking all the time. He never thought of publishing. We published his works in spite of him. He wrote only as a means of thinking. I have known many famous men, but no one has impressed me as Macedonio Fernández.

AUDIENCE: Someone characterized our age as a time when humanism is of diminished importance in our arts and culture. Do you consider yourself to be a humanist and would you comment on this hypothesis?

BORGES: I think we should do our best to save humanism. It is the one thing we have. I do what I can. I think of myself as a humanist, of course. I take no interest whatsoever in, say, politics, in money making, in fame—all those things are alien to me. But of course I worship Virgil, I worship all literatures. I worship the past—we need it in order to create the future. Yes, I think in terms of the decline of the West, as Spengler had it, but we may be saved, for all I know, by the Far East, by Japan, for example. We should try to do our own saving of ourselves. That would be better.

AUDIENCE: What do you think of the future of literature?

BORGES: I think that literature is quite safe. Literature is a necessity of the human mind.

6

But I Prefer Dreaming

Massachusetts Institute of
Technology, April 1980

I think I am concerned with images rather
than with ideas. I am not capable of abstract
thinking. Even of what the Greeks did and
what the Hebrews did, I tend to think not in
terms of reason but of fables and metaphors.
That's my stock in trade. Of course I have
to reason now and then. I do it in a very
clumsy way. But I prefer dreaming.

JAIME ALAZRAKI: Could you clarify your own debt to the English language?

JORGE LUIS BORGES: I think the chief event in my life has been my father's library. Therein I did most of my reading. The library was composed of English books. My father knew by heart ever so many stanzas by Keats, by Shelley, by Swinburne. He knew by heart Fitzgerald's *Rubiyat.* And I also remember him intoning verses of Poe. And some of them have stuck to me since that time. Poetry came to me through the English language. Afterwards it came to me through the Spanish language, especially in the verses I did not understand—after all, understanding is not important.

As I say, I felt poetry without understanding it when I was a boy. And it came to me through my father. And my mother, who died five years ago, used to say that when I intoned British verses, especially when I intoned stanzas of Swinburne, of Keats, I was going over them with my dead father's voice.

BARNSTONE: At the very beginning of Dante's *Vita Nuova,* Dante speaks of copying a dictation given to him from his own memory. He writes: "In my book of memory, in the early part, where there is little to read, there comes a chapter with the rubric *Incipit vita nova.* It is my intention to copy into this little book the words I find written under that

79

heading, if not all of them at least the essence of their meaning." Could you comment on what is given to you from your book of memory or from wherever you hear that voice?

BORGES: I think of writing as a dictation. Let us say, I am suddenly aware that something is about to happen. Then I sit back and try to be as passive as I can, try not to meddle with it. And then I see something. There is always an initial inspiration, a partial one. I may be given a line, I may be given a plot, or in a dream I may be given a word or certain words. For example, when I was in America in East Lansing several years ago, I had a dream. When I awoke the whole thing had been forgotten. But I retained this sentence: "I am about to sell you Shakespeare's memory." Then I woke. I told that to María Kodama, my friend, and she said to me: "There might be a story lurking there." I let it wait. I try not to meddle with what the Holy Ghost or inspiration or the muse or, as they say today, the subconscious gave me. And I then wrote the story. It's being published now in Buenos Aires. And the story's called "The Memory of Shakespeare." But in my story the personal memory of Shakespeare is not sold. It is merely given. It is felt in the beginning as a gift. But in the end there is something unbearable about it. And the man is disappearing under the weight of Shakespeare's personal memory.

KENNETH BRECHER: In physics we are constantly trying to reduce the world of complex phenomena to simple principles, to a few principles. But in all your writings you seem to be proving the immense complexity of the universe, which confounds our attempt to unravel it, and yet you seem to have the point of view that the universe is essentially complex, irreducible, and that man's attempts will ultimately fail. Is this a correct representation of your view of the world? What is your world view?

BORGES: If any. I think of the world as a riddle. And the one beautiful thing about it is that it can't be solved. But of course I think the world needs a riddle. I feel amazement all the time. For example, I was born way back in Buenos Aires in 1899 and here I am in America, ringed in by friends. All this is unbelievable, and yet it's true. At least I suppose it is true. Or maybe I'm not here, for all I know.

ALAZRAKI: You have given several lectures in Argentina on the subject of—

BORGES: Far too many.

ALAZRAKI: Well, not really. On a particular subject which I know

interests you, on the subject of the Kabbalah. You have also published
on this subject, early in 1926 when you included that essay "A Study of
Angels" in *El tamaño de mi esperanza, The Size of My Hope*. Now your
fiction—

BORGES: I am thoroughly ashamed of that book, but go ahead, yes. I
try to forget it. A very poor book.

ALAZRAKI: I know you don't like it.

BORGES: No. Let's avoid unpleasant subjects.

ALAZRAKI: I know you even went to the extreme of going around
Buenos Aires, gathering copies of that book.

BORGES: And burning them. That was an act of justice.

ALAZRAKI: Still, there are several essays in that book which I'm sure
you consider redeemable.

BORGES: I have never reread that book. Or any of my books, for that
matter. I write but I don't reread.

ALAZRAKI: But what that book shows, at least, is your very early
interest in the Kabbalah, and your fiction and poetry are crisscrossed with
references to it. What does the Kabbalah mean to you?

BORGES: I suppose the Kabbalah means much to me since I think I
come of Jewish stock. My mother's name was Acevedo, another in her
family was Pinedo. Those are Sephardic Jews. But also I find a very
interesting idea in the Kabbalah, the idea that Carlysle and Leon Bloch
had also. It is that the whole world is merely a system of symbols, that
the whole world, including the stars, stood for God's secret writing. That
idea is to be found in the Kabbalah and I think that that may be the
chief attraction to it. I've read many books on the Kabbalah. I should
advise you to read—but who am I to advise anybody—Gershom
Scholem's *Major Trends of Jewish Mysticism*. It's quite the best intro-
duction to the subject. I knew Scholem in Jerusalem. He sent me another
book on the golem. The first book I ever read in German was Meyerig's
novel *Der Golem*. I read it through and therein I found that idea which
always attracted me, the idea of the double. As they say in Scotland, the
"fetch," because the fetch is your own image that comes to fetch you and
lead you to death. While in German the word *Doppelgänger* is used. It
means the man, the invisible man, who walks by your side and who is
like yourself. The idea of course of Jekyll and Hyde, *The Picture of
Dorian Gray*, Alex Arner, and so on. But really, since I don't know
Hebrew I wonder if I have any right to study the Kabbalah. Yet I go

on studying it, for my pleasure. I use the word *pleasure,* and happiness, after all, should not be sneezed at.

BARNSTONE: Borges, I wanted to ask a similar question on the gnostics and your notion of otherness.

BORGES: Otherness is a good word. You made it up of course.

BARNSTONE: In the gnostic texts there are certain notions which you may wish to comment on.

BORGES: Well, altruism is the same word.

BARNSTONE: Specifically, the author Marcion speaks of the other, alien God, the unknown, the nameless Father or Mother. This alien or other life is the true life as the alien God is the true God. And the goal of the gnostic is the release of the inner person from the bonds of this world, from the mistake of this world, so that he or she can return to the real life.

BORGES: To find the *pleroma,* I think is the word.

BARNSTONE: Pleroma, right, the divine realm with its thirty divine characteristics. Would you elaborate those gnostic ideas of otherness, of mistaken worlds, salvation through escape from this world into light, into the other world?

BORGES: I suppose life, I suppose the world, is a nightmare, but I can't escape from it and am still dreaming it. And I cannot reach salvation. It's shielded from us. Yet I do my best and I find my salvation to be the act of writing, of going in for writing in a rather hopeless way. What can I do? I'm over eighty. I am blind. I am very often lonely. What else can I do but go on dreaming, then writing, then, in spite of what my father told me, rushing into print. That's my fate. My fate is to think of all things, of all experiences, as having been given me for the purpose of making beauty out of them. I know that I have failed, I'll keep on failing, but still that is the only justification of my life. To go on experiencing things, to go on being happy, being sad, being perplexed, being puzzled—I am always puzzled by things and then I try to make poetry out of those experiences. And of the many experiences, the happiest is reading. Ah, there is something far better than reading, and that is rereading, going deeper into it because you have read it, enriching it. I should advise people to read little but to reread much.

BRECHER: Would you say that in your philosophical stories and essays you are creating images or describing the metaphysical ideas themselves? Is the language the dominant feature or the philosophical notions?

BORGES: I think I am concerned with images rather than with ideas. I am not capable of abstract thinking. Even of what the Greeks did and what the Hebrews did, I tend to think not in terms of reason but of fables and metaphors. That's my stock in trade. Of course I have to reason now and then. I do it in a very clumsy way. But I prefer dreaming. I prefer images. Or as Kipling had it, a writer may be allowed to write down a fable, but, as to the moral of the fable, that may be unknown to him and may be different. So that I try to go on dreaming, try to use metaphor or fables rather than arguments. I always think the other man is in the right.

AUDIENCE: The Old English epic *Beowulf* and various Old Norse sagas present heroes who are idealized models of social conduct while simultaneously suggesting contradictions inherent in such social systems, for example, the inevitability of blood feuds, the heroes placing reckless courage over pragmatic consideration, et cetera. Do you think it's possible for contemporary literature to achieve the same effect?

BORGES: I should answer that I know that it can, since we have the epic sense in such works as Bernard Shaw's *Caesar and Cleopatra,* in such works as *The Seven Pillars of Wisdom* by Lawrence. Therein I find the epic. I was always more touched by the epic than by the lyric side of poetry. I think we may achieve the epic. Why think that that great form of art has been denied us? But of course we have to look for it in a different way. Perhaps the epic may not be wrought today in verse, but surely can be wrought in prose. I have given you a few examples and of course there are many. For example, Whitman saw *Leaves of Grass* as being an epic, not as being a series of short poems. And he was right, since he created that great mythical figure we call Walt Whitman. So I think that epic is not denied us. Nothing is forbidden us. It depends on us to do it or at least attempt it.

ALAZRAKI: Since the subject of poetry was touched upon, I'd like to turn to your poetry. In the last eleven years you have published five of your most important collections of poetry: *Elogio de la sombra, In Praise of Darkness* (1969), *El oro de los tigres, The Gold of the Tigers* (1972), *La rosa profunda, The Deep Rose* (1975), *La moneda de hierro, The Iron Coin* (1976), and *Historia de la noche, History of the Night* (1977).

BORGES: *Historia de la noche.* The pick of the bunch. The best one.

ALAZRAKI: In less than ten years you have more than tripled your poetic production.

BORGES: So I have. I should apologize to you all!

ALAZRAKI: Some readers and critics see in those collections some of the most accomplished and intense poetry you ever wrote.

BORGES: You are very generous. Go ahead.

ALAZRAKI: But it is your feeling that in these last years you find poetry a more fitting and effective medium than prose. Why is it that you have turned so vividly and intensely to poetry and slowly have almost abandoned prose?

BORGES: I don't think I have abandoned prose. I have written *Dr. Brodie's Report* and *The Book of Sand.* Those are my best short stories. But a case may be made for what my friend Alazraki has said. The fact is that since I am blind, since I am often lonely, well, it is easier to compose a rough mental draft of verse than of prose. That is to say, I am alone and then a line comes to me, and yet another. I go on polishing those lines. I remember them by heart because of the rhymes. So that poetry comes in an easier way to me. Now, had I a secretary, things might be different. I might dictate many things to him. But I haven't. And of course the one great advantage of poetry is that when you write prose you tend to see part of what you are writing, but if you write a poem, then you can see the whole. For example, a sonnet can be seen by the poet. It is composed of fourteen lines and those lines can be looked at in a single glimpse, while a narrative may be long, may be seven pages. So I find it easier to compose poetry than prose. Well, that's my personal case. Plus the fact of being blind, of being obliged to evolve rough mental drafts. The drafts are not pages. So in that case I should say that the creating is a physical one. The fact of being blind, and of being, well, sometimes lonely and by myself. But I have in mind many stories that I would write. I know the plots already. I haven't gone into details as yet, but I expect to write at least one more book of short stories. And maybe I'll go on writing verse, and when I have some thirty or forty they'll be collected into a volume like the others.

BARNSTONE: Is there any particular reason why you decide to write a poem in free verse or in traditional rhyme?

BORGES: I suppose the first line given me is the clue. If I'm given an eleven-syllable line, then that forebodes a sonnet. If I'm given a line of free verse, I go on in free verse.

BRECHER: In *Garden of the Forking Paths* the instructor of the labyrinth Ts'ui Pên writes the following:

In contrast to Newton and Schopenhauer, your ancestor did not believe in uniform, absolute time. He believed in an infinite series of times, in a growing, dizzying net of divergent, convergent, and parallel times. The network of times which approached one another, forked, broke off, or were unaware of one another for centuries embraces *all* possibilities of time.

BORGES: Yes, I think I took that from Bradley's *Appearance of Reality.* I cribbed it. It may be true for all I know. The world is so mysterious and so rich. For I found that idea while thinking of Bradley's *Appearance and Reality.* And there is another book, Dunne's *Experiment with Time,* which might be quoted. And in Schopenhauer there is a remark on the subject many times, not necessarily present, past, or to come, but altogether different.

BRECHER: Along this line, in *The Book of Sand,* you begin a story here in Cambridge during your last visit. It begins: "It was in Cambridge I sat down on the bench, facing the Charles River."

BORGES: Ah yes, I remember, yes.

BRECHER: You wrote that story?

BORGES: Yes, that story is called "The Other" I think. Remember Barnstone's "otherness"?

BRECHER: Have you ever sat on a bench and met a future Borges as opposed to a young Borges? And if so, what did he tell you?

BORGES: No. I cannot yet. But I thought of that. I'll write that story down.

BRECHER: Can you tell us the story?

BORGES: It's not yet written. I attempted it and I failed. I'll try again.

BARNSTONE: You often speak of death with expectation and hope. Do you feel no fear or anger? Could you say something about the time, or non-time, of death?

BORGES: When I am unhappy—and I allow myself to be unhappy now and then—I think of death as the great salvation. After all, what on earth can it matter what happens to Jorge Luis Borges? I'll see him no more. I think of death as a hope, a hope to be totally blotted out, obliterated, and I can count on that, and I know that there is no future life, no cause for fear or for hope. We shall simply vanish and that's as it should be. I think of immortality as being a threat, but in fact it will never achieve anything. I am sure that I am not personally immortal. And I feel that death will prove a happiness, since what better thing can we expect than forgetfulness, oblivion? That's the way I feel about it.

AUDIENCE: Since you are such a peaceful man, why is there so much violence in your stories?

BORGES: Perhaps because I come of military stock. Because I might have been somebody else. But really, now, I don't believe it. I don't believe in violence, I don't believe in war. I think the whole thing is a mistake. I believe in agreeing, not in disagreeing. I don't believe in countries. Countries are a mistake, are a superstition. I suppose the world should be one, even as the stoics thought. We should be cosmopolitans, citizens of the world. I have so many hometowns, for example, Buenos Aires, for example, Austin, Texas, for example, Montivideo, well, tonight Cambridge, why not? Geneva, Edinburgh, ever so many hometowns. It's much better than having one hometown or one country.

AUDIENCE: You didn't mention William Butler Yeats among the poets you like.

BORGES: Well, I should of course. I am very sorry for that omission. I apologize to all of you. Yeats is a great poet but, I should say, I'm not sure if his is a lasting poetry, since what you chiefly get from him is surprise. And surprise fades away. I think that Frost will last longer than Yeats. Of course I delight in Yeats. I can give you so many lines from him. At this moment a line bubbles up. The line is thus: "That dolphin-torn, that gong-tormented sea." What wonderful baroque verse. I'm not very fond of baroque verse. While Frost wrote many verses that go deeper down than it.

AUDIENCE: Is the story "Funes the Memorious" autobiographical?

BORGES: Yes. It is. It is meant as a metaphor for insomnia. I remember I had very sleepless nights, and then I did my best to forget myself, to forget the room I was in, to forget the garden outside the room, to forget the furniture, to forget the many facts of my own body, and I couldn't do it. And I thought of a man being weighed down by a perfect memory. Then I wrote that nightmare that has pleased many people, called "Funes the Memorious." Essentially, *memorious* in English is a farfetched word while in Spanish *memorioso* sounds like a plain word. So the title in this case is better in translation. *Memorioso* sounds almost as if it had been said by a peasant. Well, the story itself is, though I wrote it, a fine story.

Audience: Some people wonder why you have never written a full-length novel. Do you believe the forms you use are superior to the novel form? And why?

Borges: I should say for merely personal reasons. The reason is that I *can't* write a novel, though I can write short stories, and that's that.

Audience: Some people are wondering about the translations of your work. Are people allowed to retranslate works of yours that have already been translated?

Borges: Norman Thomas de Giovanni told me that his translations were far better than the originals. He was right, I suppose. I'm being improved and invented all the time by my translators. Among them, of course, Willis Barnstone and Alastair Reid. They are improving me all the time. They should be as unfaithful as they can. They are of course.

Margery Resnick: Are there more questions?

Borges: Life is brief. I'm eighty-one. I may die at any moment. Go ahead.

Audience: Are you acquainted with Diderot?

Borges: Of course I am.

Audience: Could you talk of how you view *seguro azar* ["unavoidable chance"] and how does this fit in with fatalism as Diderot sees it?

Borges: I wonder if I can answer that very complex question. Personally, I think that free will is an illusion, but a necessary illusion. For example, if I am told my past has been given me, I accept it. Whereas if I am told that I am not a free agent now, I can't believe in it. So that free will is a necessary illusion. Of course Spinoza knew all about that when he said a stone falling could think "I want to fall." I think that if I want to go on writing I am made to think so, not by any god, but by that long chain of causes and effects, branching out into infinity.

Audience: Could you explain your idea of poetic inspiration?

Borges: I know that the thing exists and that's all I knew about it. I know that I am given gifts and I misuse them. But I know inspiration exists. Where it comes from I don't know. It may come from memory, from an unknown agent. But I know inspiration exists and all poets know it. Even as I know that the experience of yellow exists, that the experience of love exists, the experience of inspiration exists. That's all I know about it. And we need know no more.

Audience: Could you speak about recitation? We wonder what you feel about oral literature when oral engagement with literature is under attack from the printed word.

BORGES: When a poem is a real poem, the reader has to read it up aloud. That's the test of poetry. In reading a poem, or for that matter a novel or a short tale, if you don't feel that you'd better read it up aloud, then there is something wrong about the writing. I notice many times over that though literature may be written, it is essentially oral. Since it began by being oral, it goes on being oral.

AUDIENCE: What should the role of the artist be in a society as threatened as ours? Can beauty survive in the ambience in which we find ourselves?

BORGES: I think that poetry and beauty will prevail. I have no use for politics. I am not politically minded. I am aesthetically minded, philosophically perhaps. I don't belong to any party. In fact, I disbelieve in politics and in nations. I disbelieve also in richness, in poverty. Those things are illusions. But I believe in my own destiny as a good or bad or indifferent writer.

7

A Writer Is Waiting
for His Own Work

Indiana University,
March 1976

If you allow me to be paradoxical—and
why not since we are among friends?—a
writer is waiting for his own work. I think
a writer is being changed all the time by
his output. So that perhaps at first what he
writes is not relevant to him. And if he
goes on writing, he'll find that those things
are ringing a bell all the time.

WILLIS BARNSTONE: During World War I, when you were in
Geneva, studying in French and Latin, talking English and Spanish at
home, you came upon another American poet whose lines you read in
German: *Als ich in Alabama meinen Morgengang machte.*

JORGE LUIS BORGES: Walt Whitman.

BARNSTONE: What effect did finding that other American have upon
the possibility of a modern language for your poetry?

BORGES: When I read Walt Whitman, I did not think of myself as a
poet. I read it as a reader, and I was swept off my feet. I thought that
Walt Whitman was perhaps the only poet, that all other poets, from
Homer and so on down to Whitman, were merely his forerunners. That
was the sensation I got. The same sensation that I had when I first discovered Hugo, John Donne, or why not Seneca? who was also a poet, or
Shakespeare, or Quevedo.

I suppose the first time a young man discovers a poet he thinks of him
not as a poet but as poetry, as poetry as an art at last discovered by someone
after the gropings of the centuries. That was the impression I got from
Whitman. I said what bunglers all the others have been. Now I see of
course that I was wrong, since all poets are right in their way, and I don't
think that one should think of one as being an outstanding poet. In fact,

I suspect that poetry is not an uncommon thing. I suppose that even the worst poets, I myself for example, may have achieved a fine verse now and then. In every book of some third-rate Argentine writer there may be a fine verse. And perhaps God, if he exists—of course he may not exist—would certainly think that every moment *is* wonderful, otherwise why on earth should this poetry writing be going on.

SCOTT SANDERS: You have said that you are a literary man, not a thinker, not a philosopher. And yet those of us who read you, and there are millions who read you, get great joy and excitement from the conceptual quality, the intellectual quality of your writing. Are we misreading you?

BORGES: No, I think that you are enriching me. Because after all reading is an elaboration even as experience is an elaboration. Every time I read something, that something is changed. And every time I write something, that something is being changed all the time by every reader. Every new experience enriches the book. You can see that—I am thinking of the Bible—you can see how it has been enriched through the many generations. I suppose Hamlet is a far richer character after Coleridge than he was for Shakespeare who created him. Yet for myself, I know I am not a thinker, except in the sense of being very puzzled over things. I try to find interpretations and I generally find them by letting the author do my thinking for me, that is to say, in Hume and Berkeley and Schopenhauer and Bradley and William James, and the Greeks also. But I think that I use thinking for literary purposes. I think of myself primarily as being a man of letters. I have acquired, at long last, some skill in the writing of Spanish, not too much, but I can more or less express what I want to, and I can say it in fairly melodious language. But then people read my stories and read many things into them that I have not intended, which means that I am a writer of stories. A writer who wrote only the things he intended would be a very poor writer. A writer should write with a certain innocence. He shouldn't think about what he is doing. If not, what he does is not at all his own poetry.

ROBERT DUNN: Do you think that there is a proper relationship of the personality of the writer to his product? That is, what distance should be established between the latter and the former?

BORGES: If you allow me to be paradoxical—and why not since we are among friends?—a writer is waiting for his own work. I think a writer is being changed all the time by his output. So that perhaps at first what he writes is not relevant to him. And if he goes on writing, he'll find that those things are ringing a bell all the time. I have written far more than I should have written. I am sorry to say that I have written fifty or sixty books, and yet I find all those books are contained in the first book I ever published, in that dim book, written ever so long ago, *Fervor de Buenos Aires,* published way back in 1923. That book is a book of poems, and yet I find that most of my stories are there, except that they are there lurking, they are to be found there in a secret way and only I can ferret them out. And yet I keep on rereading that book and reshaping what I have written in that book. That is all I can do now. Some character in a Western says: "You are mute and dim." But I go back to that book and there I find myself, and there I find my future books.

BARNSTONE: In various conversations and so frequently in your writing you mention Milton. You mention him far more than you do Dante. And yet I have the feeling that you perhaps appreciate Dante more than you do Milton. Could you tell us something about why you like Dante? What is it in Dante?

BORGES: Had I to name a single work as being at the top of all literature, I think I should choose the *Divina Commedia* by Dante. And yet I am not a Catholic. I cannot believe in theology. I cannot believe in the idea of punishment or of reward. Those things are alien to me. But the poem in itself is perfect. Not the last part of the poem, since no man can imagine he is dead because he is in hell all the time. Now in the case of Dante, you can hear that every line is perfect. While Milton is lofty but also rather tame. And besides, I cannot be fond of Milton personally. In the case of Dante, I wonder if I *am* fond of him. But I think of him as being a real man. I can hardly think of Milton as being a real man. For example, it is very clear to me that when Dante had his dream of hell and his dream of purgatory, he was imagining things, but in the case of Milton he was working rather in terms of words, not images. Now, you may say, that for a poet, that kind of thinking should be allowed. It is. But it does not touch me as Dante touches me. I am impressed by Milton. But I am *only* impressed by him. But as for Dante, I feel every word standing out. I think of every image as being exactly as it should be. You don't have to justify his lines. You don't have to think of him in terms of the Middle Ages. Every word is perfect, every word is in its place. You think nobody could better a line of Dante. While there are many lines of Milton that I, at least, think are quite wretched. If you have to admire Milton—why should we not?—I should think of *Samson Agonistes* and of the sonnets rather than of *Paradise Lost* or *Paradise Regained*. *Paradise Regained* is quite bad. And even if it is *Paradise Lost,* I cannot accept the theology. I cannot accept the story, for example, of God making man and then making Christ. All those things are beyond me. They really are. But in the case of the sonnets, of course he wrote some very powerful sonnets. In fact, I suppose that except for the fact that they both wrote of God, of hell and of heaven, there is no link whatever between Milton and Dante. They are really quite unlike each other, and I wonder why we link them together. What I am saying is very obvious, and obvious things are very trivial.

ROGER CUNNINGHAM: On the story "The Sect of the Phoenix," right at the beginning you have somebody quote the doctrine of some obscure gnostic sect—it's always good to have an obscure gnostic sect.

BORGES: Oh yes, of course. They're very handy, eh? They're available at any moment.

CUNNINGHAM: That somebody says that mirrors and copulation are both abominable because they increase the number of persons.

BORGES: I am those obscure gnostics!

CUNNINGHAM: To ask a dull question of fact, what have you read in gnosticism, firsthand, like the Poimandres or any of those nice things?

BORGES: I have read a book by a man called Hans Leisegang, called *Die Gnosis.* Then a book by an Englishman called Mead, which I read in a German translation, *Fragmente Forschungen.* Then I have read some translations from the *Glaubens Pistis Sophia.* So that I give you Leisegang, I give you Mead, I give you Deussen's *Geschichte der Philosophie.* And then another book written by a German theologian. I read that in 1918, but then I lost the book. That's all I know about it really. And that was sufficient for my own South American literary purposes.

AUDIENCE: Would you like to tell us about the use of violence in your short stories?

BORGES: I think the use of violence can be attributed to the fact that my grandfather fell in action, and my great-grandfather won a battle, in the cavalry charge in Peru in 1856. Those people always had a kind of hankering for what we might call an epic history. Of course I was denied that, since I don't think I would have made a good soldier, especially by reason of my defective eyesight. So I have a tendency to think of things in that way. And then somehow my friends are hoodlums, who go in for knives. The gauchos also. And those things have stood me without myself fighting. After all, I don't think you should worry about that fact, since every writer is free to choose his own symbols. If I have chosen, let us say, miller, masons, and knives, why not? Why should I not be allowed to do so?

AUDIENCE: Could you tell us about your story "El Sur," "The South," how you conceived it, how it came about?

BORGES: I had been reading Henry James. I was greatly struck, as you all have been, by that story "The Turn of the Screw," which admits of several interpretations. You might think of the apparitions as being fiends masquerading as ghosts, and you might think of the children as being fools, or as being victims or perhaps accomplices. Henry James has written several stories rolled into one. Then I thought I would do the same thing myself. I would try the same trick by writing three stories at a time. Then I wrote "El Sur." In "El Sur," you will find three stories. You have firstly that of parody. There is a man being killed by the thing he loves. That is the reverse of what Oscar Wilde said: "For each man kills the thing he loves." That would be one version. Another would be if you read the story as being realistic. Then you also might have the most interesting interpretation, which doesn't exclude the others: you might think of the second half of the story as being what the man was dreaming when he died under the knife in the hospital. Because, really, that man was hungering after an epic death. He was inclined to die in the sharpness of the blades with a knife in his hand. He was actually dying under the surgeon's knife. So all that was dreamt up by him. I have the feeling that that was the interpretation. Really I think that story is a good story technically, because I tell those three stories at once, at one time. And they don't intrude on each other. That's what makes it interesting. You might have at first a parable. A man is thirsting for the south and when he goes back to the south, the south kills him. There you have the parable. Then the realistic story of the man going insane and of being made to fight with a drunken murderer. Then the third, which is the best, I think, that the whole thing is a dream. So the story would be not the actual death of the man, but the one he dreamt of while he was dying.

AUDIENCE: Is poetry "a sweet vengeance against life"?

BORGES: I can hardly agree to that. I think of poetry as being an essential part of life. How could it be against life? Poetry is perhaps *the* essential part of life. I do not think of life, or of reality, as lying beyond me or outside of me. I *am* life, I am *within* life. And one of the many facts of life is language and words and poetry. Why should I pit them one against the other?

AUDIENCE: But the *word* life is not life.

BORGES: But life, I suppose, might be the sum total, if such a sum total be possible, of *all* things, and then, why not language also? I cannot think of life as being something outside me, of being something very different. Since I am living, what else can I do? But I am also living when I dream, when I sleep, when I write, when I read. I am living all the time. If I consider my past experiences, I suppose Swinburne is as much a part of my experience as the life I led in Geneva in 1917. All those things are part of my experience. I have no need to classify it, or to think of life as different from me. In the case of Alonso Quijano, I suppose the chief event in his life was the reading of the chivalric romance *Amadis de gaula* and he became a very real Don Quixote. I don't think of life as being pitted against literature. I believe that art is a part of life.

AUDIENCE: Which writers of today interest you?

BORGES: The writers of today who interest me are chiefly dead writers. I'm an old man. I may be a dead man for all I know.

AUDIENCE: I would like to rephrase a question that was asked earlier about the relationship between the personality and the work. I came across a remark made by Flaubert: "The man is nothing, the work is everything." I think of the story "The Three Versions of Judas" and the possibility that in taking on a great work of any kind the work can be in opposition to the man.

BORGES: I am hampered by the fact that I can't remember that story. I wrote it and have utterly forgotten it. That I wrote three versions suggests three different examples of the same subject. I cannot even remember it. But I suppose there *has* to be a link between a writer and his work. Otherwise the work would be a combination of words, a mere game.

AUDIENCE: Could you compare Buenos Aires today with the past?

BORGES: Today Buenos Aires hardly exists, I am sorry to say. My country is breaking down. I feel very sad about things. When I think of my childhood I feel very happy. I think of people as being happier than they are today. Today I know nothing of Buenos Aires. I don't understand it. I can only feel puzzled and saddened by what is happening or what is going on in my country. But I love it because, after all, my country right or wrong. I know that I am homesick for that anarchy, since that anarchy stands for so many things in my life. And I also think of my country not in terms of politics or the economy, but in terms of a few fine friendships, and habits. The habit of friendship is profoundly important to me.

MIGUEL ENGUÍDANOS: Borges, as you will remember, a few years ago we had a conversation in which you told me something very puzzling. You said: "I am going to abandon literature."

BORGES: Did I?

ENGUÍDANOS: Yes, you said that.

BORGES: Now that puzzles *me*.

ENGUÍDANOS: Let me explain the circumstances. We were in Oklahoma. Supposedly you had in mind prospecting for oil or something.

BORGES: Yes, that's my habit! I'm always doing it.

ENGUÍDANOS: And then you told me that you were going to devote the rest of your life to the study of Spinoza and the Old Norse sagas. The truth of the matter is that since then you have been not only as productive as ever but you have produced some of your most remarkable poetry and short stories. Now the main question is this: Will you be kind enough to tell us what Borges is doing now?

BORGES: I am sorry to say I am writing poems and tales. I also intend to write a book on Swedenborg, not on Spinoza. They both begin with *S*, however.

ENGUÍDANOS: Yes, but will you explain to me what it means, your nostalgia for that key, or that door in Buenos Aires?

BORGES: It means that after all I am an Argentine, a mere Argentine, so I feel homesick, though I feel very happy in America.

ENGUÍDANOS: No, no, excuse me, you are evading the question. I am not trying to trick you. Do you have any statement about your present aesthetics or your present poetics, if you want to tell us?

BORGES: No, I am sorry to say I have no aesthetics. I can only *write* poetry and tales. I have no theory. I don't think theories are any good, really.

BARNSTONE: You could devastate half a university with that last comment.

AUDIENCE: How does dictating poems and stories now affect your creative problems?

BORGES: I think it's a great help. I don't have to be going over my handwriting. Now I just dictate, and go on. I don't have to hurry. Dictating lines may be difficult, for all I know. But at least now I feel at home in it. Besides I have friends who are very kind and very patient. I can do my work as I like. But I don't feel that being blind and having to dictate as being necessarily an evil.

BARNSTONE: Would you say something about friendship? You speak about it so much.

BORGES: I think friendship is perhaps *the* essential fact of life. Friendship, as Adolpho Bioy Casares said to me, has this advantage over love, in that it needs no proofs whatever. In the case of love, you are always worrying about being loved or not, and you are always in a sad state of mind, in a state of anxiety, whereas in friendship you may not have seen a friend for a year or so. He may have slighted you. He may have tried to avoid you. But if you are his friend, and you know that he is your friend, then you don't have to worry about that. Friendship, once it is established, needs nothing. It just goes on. There is something magical, there is a kind of spell about friendship. And I'd say that perhaps the one virtue that may be allowed my most unhappy country is the virtue of friendship. And I think that Barnstone here should know something about it. I think that he knows that friendship means much to us. In fact, when the poet Eduardo Mallea wrote a fine book called *Historia de una Pasión Argentina, History of an Argentine Passion,* I said to myself, this must be friendship, for it is the only passion that we really have. And then I went on and found it was a mere love story and I was quite disappointed.

AUDIENCE: Señor Borges, do you believe that poetry exists only in books?

BORGES: No. I think poetry, as I said, is existing all the time, except that we are not sensitive to it. Poetry of course grows in memory. My memory is full of verses. But there are also situations that are poetic. But why should it exist only in books? After all, books only exist when they are being read and when they are being remembered. Is not a book a thing among things? Why should we take it seriously? Why should we stand in awe of a bound volume? There is no reason whatever. I suppose poetry exists beyond the words, since the words are mere chance symbols. Poetry exists in the music of words.

AUDIENCE: You mentioned Don Quixote before in passing and I wanted to ask you if you would care to comment on *Don Quixote?*

BORGES: *Don Quixote* is perhaps one of the finest books ever written. Not because of the plot—the plot is flimsy, the episodes go nowhere—but the man, Alonso Quijano, who dreamt himself into Don Quixote is perhaps one of our best friends. At least he is my best friend. Creating a friend for the many generations to come is a feat which could hardly be equaled. And Cervantes has done that.

8

Time Is
the Essential Mystery

University of Chicago,
March 1980

I think that time is the one essential mystery. Other things may be mysterious. Space is unimportant. You can think of a spaceless universe, for example, a universe made of music. . . . The problem of time involves the problem of ego, for, after all, what is the ego? The ego is the past, the present, and also the anticipation of time to come, of the future.

WILLIS BARNSTONE: Borges, although you are almost blind, you always remark on the qualities of the rooms and buildings you are in. How do you see with your limited eyes, and how do you feel here today in this hall?

JORGE LUIS BORGES: I feel friendship. I feel a very real welcome. Liked by people, loved by people, I feel all that. I don't feel the circumstances but the essential, way down. I don't know how I do it, but I'm sure that I am right.

BARNSTONE: You often compare friendship with love. Would you be willing to make a comparison between friendship and love?

BORGES: Love is a very strange thing, full of misgivings, full of hope, and those things may make for happiness. But in friendship there is no misleading, no hope, the thing goes on and on. There's no need of frequency, we do not need tokens. But we know that if we are friends, and the other person is a friend, perhaps in the long run friendship is more important than love. Or perhaps the true function, the duty of love, is to become friendship. If not, it stops us halfway. But both should be greatly loved.

BARNSTONE: Would you speak of experience and poetry?

BORGES: I think that to a poet (and sometimes I think of myself in that way), all things are given for the purpose of being turned into poetry. So that unhappiness is not really unhappiness. Unhappiness is a tool that is given us, even as a knife may be a tool. All experience should become poetry, and if we were really poets (and I'm not really a poet. I pretend to be a poet), but if I were really a poet, I would think of every moment in life as being beautiful, even though at the moment it may not seem so. But in the end, memory turns all things into beauty. Our task, our duty, is to turn emotions, recollections, even memories of sad things into beauty. That is our task. And the great advantage of that task is that we never attain it. We are always on the point of doing it.

BARNSTONE: In "The Parable of the Prince" from *Dreamtigers*—

BORGES: I wish I could remember it.

BARNSTONE: Memories are to be forgotten.

BORGES: It's utterly forgotten.

BARNSTONE: The parable ends with the poet's descendants still looking for the one word which contains the universe. Are you seeking one word, a state of mind, a feeling, an understanding? What is it that you seek— if anything—before you die?

BORGES: I suppose the only way of finding the right word is not to look for it. One should live in the present moment. Then afterwards the words may be given us or they may not. We have to go on, by trial and error. We have to make our mistakes, we have to unmake them. And that of course is a lifelong job.

BARNSTONE: You do not believe in a personal god, yet lacking other symbols or analogies you often use the word *god* in your poems. Do you believe in anything or look for anything that eludes causality, in anything that is transcendental?

BORGES: Of course I do. I believe in the mystery of the world. When people use the word *god,* I think of what George Bernard Shaw said. He said, if I remember rightly: "God is in the making." And we are the makers. We are begetting God. We are creating God every time that we attain beauty. As for rewards and punishments, those things are mere threats and bribes. I have no use for them. I don't believe in a personal god. But why should a personal god be more important than a god that is—I am in a pantheistic mood today—all of us? We are all in a sense God. And I think I am an ethical man, or I have done my best to be an ethical man. I think that I have acted rightly and that should be enough also. I cannot believe in a personal god. I've done my best to believe in a personal god, but I can't. And yet my forefathers were Methodist preachers, I'm sorry to say. My grandmother knew her Bible by heart; she knew chapter and verse. But she also knew Dickens by heart. That's quite as good.

BARNSTONE: You've guessed my next question. What do you want to tell us about Dickens?

BORGES: When one thinks of Dickens, one thinks really of a crowd. I say "Dickens" but I think of Mr. Pickwick, of the Artful Dodger, of Nicholas Nickolby, of Martin Chuzzlewit and the murder in *Martin Chuzzlewit*. I think of Dickens, and then I'm really thinking of a crowd of men. As to Dickens himself, he is not as interesting as his dreams. That, of course, is meant to be in praise of Dickens. In the same way, when I say "Shakespeare," I'm not thinking of the man William Shakespeare. I am thinking of Macbeth, of the Weird Sisters, of Hamlet, and the mysterious man behind the sonnets. So in the case of Dickens, I think of many men. And those many men, who were merely the dreams of Dickens, have given me much happiness. I go on reading and rereading them.

BARNSTONE: Returning to the question of a personal god, are you a gnostic?

BORGES: I am an agnostic.

BARNSTONE: No, a *gnostic*.

BORGES: Ah yes, I may be. Why not be gnostics today and agnostics tomorrow? It's all the same thing.

BARNSTONE: And the basis of your ethics?

BORGES: I suppose at every moment of our lives we have to choose. We have to act one way or another. As Dr. Johnson had it, we are moralists all the time, not astronomers or botanists.

BARNSTONE: How, among all people, did you happen to become Borges? Are you not surprised that existence chose you? How do you account for individual consciousness?

BORGES: I am surprised and ashamed of being Borges. I've done my best to be somebody else but I haven't been able to up till now. I don't like being Borges at all. I wish I were any single one of you.

BARNSTONE: In regard to your writing, has dictating your poems, as opposed to writing them by hand, altered the poems that you write?

BORGES: I think it has altered them for the better, because they're shorter now.

BARNSTONE: Have the people to whom you have dictated the poems —your mother, Annaliese von der Lippen, María Kodama, who is here today—

BORGES: Have they objected to them? Many a time. But I'm very stubborn. I keep on.

BARNSTONE: Have their objections and opinions affected the actual writing of the poems?

BORGES: Yes, they have. They are collaborating with me, all the time. I remember I wrote a story called "The Intruder." Two hoodlums, two brothers, kill a woman because they are jealous of each other. The one way they had to get rid of her was to knife her. I came to the last sentence. My mother was writing it down. She disliked the whole thing. She was sick and tired of hoodlums and knives. Then I came to a moment when the elder brother had to tell the younger brother that he had knifed the woman that morning. Or he had strangled her, I don't know—why go into the gory details? He had to say that, and I had to find the right words. Then I told my mother: "How on earth can he say that?" And she said: "Let me think." This was in the morning. Then, suddenly, in quite a different voice, she said: "I know what he said." Then I said: "Well, write it down." She wrote it down and I asked her to read it. She read it and those words were: "To work, brother, I killed her this morning." And she found the right words for me. The story ended. I added a sentence or so. Then she asked me not to write any more of those blood-and-thunder stories. She was sick and tired of them. But she gave me the words, and at that moment she became, in a sense, one of the characters in the story, and she believed in it. She said "I know what he said" as though the thing had actually occurred. She gave me the key word for that story called "The Intruder," perhaps the best story—or perhaps the one story I have ever written.

BARNSTONE: When you were a young man, you went north for a short time with the gauchos. Could you describe your experiences, what effect they had on you and your work?

BORGES: In 1934 I went to the borderland of Brazil and Uruguay. And therein I found the Argentine past. I found the plains, the gauchos, those things that are no longer to be found in my country. Those things were expecting me, or at least were waiting there for me. I spent some ten days there. I was rather bored, but I saw a man killed. I had never seen that before. He was an old Uruguayan herd drover. He was killed by a Negro with a revolver, who got two shots into him, and he died. And I thought, what a pity. And then I thought no more about it. But afterwards, in the many years that came after those ten days in Santa Anna do Livramento, the border of Uruguay and Brazil, the place came back to me, and I seem to be always recalling it. It is very strange. I have traveled more or less all over the world. I have seen great cities. I have seen perhaps the capital city, New York, and I have also seen London and Rome and Paris. Yet I don't know why my memory goes back to that shabby little town on the Brazilian border and, when I am writing, it seems to inspire me. And yet at the time, it was not especially interesting. The whole thing happened in memory afterwards.

BARNSTONE: When you were reading as a child, as a young person—

BORGES: I was always reading.

BARNSTONE: What were the first things that you read?

BORGES: I suppose the first book I read was Grimm's *Fairy Tales.* The best book that came out of Germany, as Chesterton had it. And then I read *Alice in Wonderland* and *Through the Looking Glass.* I've gone on reading those books since then, since 1906 or 1905. I read perhaps the finest science fiction in the world, those nightmares woven by Wells. I read *The Time Machine, The First Man on the Moon, The Island of Dr. Moreau, The Invisible Man, The Food of the Gods, The War of the Worlds.* And I also discovered that endless book, endless in many senses because it's a book that has to be long. It has to live up to its title. I read for the first time the *Arabian Nights,* in an English version of Galland's French version. Then afterwards I found my way into Edward William Lane's translation and Captain Burton's translation and Littmann's translation into German. And two years ago I read a very fine Spanish translation published by Aguilar in Mexico, by the Judeo-Andalusían writer Rafael Cansinos-Asséns. A very fine translation, perhaps the finest of them all.

I found a novel, and at first I could hardly tackle it because the language was so different. But somehow I was led to it and I kept on reading it. The book is of course Cervantes' *Don Quixote.* I read that for the first time and I've gone on reading it. I've gone on reading Wells also. Those two books by Lewis Carroll. Those books were my first reading. And also I found my way into two books that I hardly look into now because I go on reading other books by the same writer. I mean the *Just So* stories and the two jungle books by Rudyard Kipling. I love Kipling. Another book I read at the time is a book that seems to me more or less unknown, and it should be known. And that book is really two books, *Roughing It* and *The First Days in California,* by Mark Twain. And then I went on to *Huckleberry Finn.* Then the tales of Poe, and at the same time Jules Verne.

BARNSTONE: When did you read Milton's *Paradise Lost?*

BORGES: My parents went to Europe in the year 1914. They were so ignorant they didn't even know that the war would begin then. Then I got a copy of Milton's works in the Everyman's Library edition, and instead of seeing Paris—I must have been fifteen at the time—I stayed in the hotel and read *Paradise Lost, Paradise Regained, Samson Agonistes,* and the sonnets. And I don't regret it.

BARNSTONE: When you first discovered the Old English poets, what effect did that have on your own writing and on you?

BORGES: I discovered Old English poetry at a moment that might have been dramatic. And I did my best not to make it dramatic. That was the year 1955, when I lost my eyesight for reading purposes. And as I was a professor of English literature, I told my students, when will we really try to know something about the subject? And I had at home a copy of Sweet's Anglo-Saxon reader. And also a copy of the Anglo-Saxon *Chronicle.* And then we began to read, and we fell in love with two words. And those two words were the Saxon names for London and for Rome. London was called Lundenburgh. *Burgh* was the same word as *borough* or *burg,* the word you get in *burgos,* in Edinburgh, Hamburg, Gottenburg, and so on. And the name for Rome was really wonderful also, because half of it was Latin, and the other Saxon. Rome was called, by the Anglo-Saxons, Romaburgh. We fell in love with those two words, and we found a beautiful sentence in the Anglo-Saxon *Chronicle.* It said: Julius Caesar, or Julius the Caesar, was the first Roman to seek out Britain. But the sentence has a finer ring to it in Old English: *Gaius Iulius se Casere ærest Romana Brytenland gesohte.* And then we ran along a street called Perú in Buenos Aires, shouting "Iulius se Casere. . . . " And people stared at us. We did not mind. We had found beauty! Then I went on studying, and now I'm going in for Old Norse. That always happens. You begin with Old English, and, if you're lucky, you achieve Old Norse.

BARNSTONE: A few questions on fame. You now think about your fame as a possible mistake.

BORGES: Of course it is. But a very generous mistake.

BARNSTONE: When you were a young man working in a provincial Buenos Aires library, what did you think then of publication and fame, and how have your thoughts along the years changed?

BORGES: I never thought of fame. The idea of fame was alien to the Buenos Aires of my youth. For example, Leopoldo Lugones would be thought rightly to be the first poet of the Argentine Republic. I suppose his editions run to five hundred copies, and he never thought of sales. I remember having read that Emily Dickinson said that publishing was no part of a writer's destiny or career. She never published. And we all thought the same way and along the same lines. We were not writing for a minority, for a majority, or for the public. We wrote to please ourselves and to please our friends perhaps. Or perhaps we wrote because we stood in need of getting rid of some idea. Alfonso Reyes, the great Mexican writer, said to me: We publish in order not to go on emending rough drafts. And I know he was right. We publish to be rid of a book, to forget it. Once the book has appeared, then we lost all interest in it. I'm sorry to say that people have written fifty or sixty books about me. I haven't read a single one of them, since I know too much of the subject, and I'm sick and tired of it.

BARNSTONE: In your writing you say that you are not brave like your ancestors, that you are a physical coward—

BORGES: Yes, I am. My dentist knows all about it!

BARNSTONE: And your eye doctor?

BORGES: My eye doctor and my surgeon also. Everybody knows it. It's no big secret.

BARNSTONE: Yet in your public life you have always spoken out against public fashion.

BORGES: Of course!

BARNSTONE: And you have never uttered an opinion for your own benefit. On the contrary. Now, I remember that you told me once that, when a thief said to you "Your money or life," you answered "My life," and so frightened the thief that he turned and ran.

BORGES: I wanted him to kill me, and he didn't want to.

BARNSTONE: Now, Borges, are you a coward or a brave man?

BORGES: I think I am physically a coward, but not mentally. I have never pandered to power or to the mob. I think that I am a brave man in the serious sense of the word, not in the military sense, though my people were all military men. But I can't think of myself as being a literary man. I can't think of myself as a soldier or as a sailor or as a businessman or, worse still, as a politician!

BARNSTONE: When you were in Japan, you were impressed by very civilized monks who practice meditation in a formal way.

BORGES: In the course of meditation, one of the subjects was this: The participant should try to think that he is the Buddha. And he may be so, for all we know. Or he should try to think of nothing, and that will also help him. I was told that in a Buddhist monastery. In Japan I was being impressed all the time. Every day was a gift to me. For all we know, we may be saved by the East, especially by Japan, since Japan has two cultures: Our Western culture, its own culture, and also the luminous shadow of Chinese culture over it. It's a very lovable country. I only spent thirty days there, but I know that those days will remain long and long with me. I am looking back on them.

BARNSTONE: How do you feel about being in a country where every day is important to you?

BORGES: I felt very, very, very grateful. And I'm feeling grateful all the time in America also. People are so good and so forgiving to me. Here you are, you take me seriously. I don't take myself seriously, and I'm thankful to you, but I think you're mistaken.

BARNSTONE: What do you see when you look into yourself?

BORGES: I try not to look into myself. Or rather, as a Chicago chauffeur said ten minutes ago, I hate memory. He said those words which might have come from Seneca. A taxi driver, who had also been a soldier.

BARNSTONE: How do you feel today, perhaps sixty years later, about your early Geneva friends, Simon Jichlinski and Maurice Abramowicz? Have you kept up with them?

BORGES: Yes, I have. I met them, and half a century had elapsed, but it was of no account. I met them, we talked, we went on talking without minding the fact that half a century had elapsed, about the same things, the French Symbolists. It was a very fine experience. No word was said about the interim. We went on talking about literature, about Latin, the German language, about Yiddish.

BARNSTONE: What books do you want to write, Borges?

BORGES: I would like to write a story called "The Prize." That story was given me by a dream some ten days ago. I keep on turning it over in my mind. I know I'll write it. I would like to write a book on Swedenborg, and perhaps a few stories, and quite a sizable amount of poems. I keep on turning them over in my mind. Also I am translating Angelus Silesius with María Kodama. We are finishing the first rough draft. And then we'll go on to better things.

BARNSTONE: What is your frank opinion about the human body, which puts you to sleep, which wakes you up, which lets you breathe, which lets us die, in which your mind is always lodged? Tell us about the body.

BORGES: I think of it as a very clumsy contrivance. Milton already wondered at the fact that sight lay in what he called "those two tender orbs," the eyes. Why not see with all your body? Then we would be blind. The whole thing is very clumsily done, but it gives us delight and also, I'm sorry to say, it gives us hell. It gives us pain. Physical pain can be really unbearable. I suppose the best solution is one given by the gnostics: the idea of a rather clumsy God, God not doing very well his own job. The same idea is to be found in a very fine novel by Wells called *The Undying Fire,* the idea of God as doing his best with a rather rough, unruly material. And to go back to Bernard Shaw, God is in the making, and we are part of the making. We should be part of God.

BARNSTONE: Would you tell us something about the poems of Emily Dickinson? What do you think of Emily Dickinson among American poets?

BORGES: Emily Dickinson is the most passionate of all women who have attempted writing. At the moment I only remember these hackneyed lines—but of course they're not hackneyed, they're eternal: "Parting is all we know of heaven/ and all we need of hell." The second line is perfect. The word *need* is the perfect word in the context. She spent her life writing, forgetting what she had written, leaving rough drafts, and now she is famous, but that is unimportant of course. I think of her as if I had known her personally. I have personal regard for her, personal love for Emily Dickinson.

BARNSTONE: Among other American poets, where would you place her?

BORGES: I think that one should never use words like "the best" or "the first," since those words carry no conviction and only lead to arguments. Beauty is not something rare. We are coming across beauty all the time. For example, I know nothing whatever about Hungarian poetry, and yet I am sure that in Hungarian poetry I should find certainly a Shakespeare, a Dante, a Fray Luis de León, because beauty is common. People are creating beauty all the time. I wrote a poem on the library of Alexandria and I dedicated it to Omar, who burned it. And I made him think thus: Here is a memory of the word. Here we have all the poems, all the dreams, all the fictions of mankind. Well, I shall burn this library, the books will be ashes, because I know that in due time other men will rewrite the same books and nothing will really be lost.

BARNSTONE: Please speak to us about time.

BORGES: I think that time is the one essential mystery. Other things may be mysterious. Space is unimportant. You can think of a spaceless universe, for example, a universe made of music. We are listeners of course. But as for time, you have the one problem of definition. I remember what Saint Augustine said: "What is time? If nobody asks me, I know what it is. If I am asked, I am ignorant, I do not know." I think that the problem of time is *the* problem. The problem of time involves the problem of ego, for, after all, what is the ego? The ego is the past, the present, and also the anticipation of time to come, of the future. So those two enigmas, those two riddles, are the essential business of philosophy, and happily for us they will never be solved, so forever we can go on. We can go on making guesswork—we will call that guesswork philosophy, which is really mere guesswork. We will go on weaving theories, and being very much amused by them, and then unweaving and taking other new ones.

BARNSTONE: You have a very curious memory.

BORGES: Yes, my memory may be, for all I know, a strange memory, since I forget my past. I tend to forget circumstances, and I abound—my friends know only too well—in quotations. But my mind is enriched. I can give you ever so many verses in Spanish, in English, in Old English, in Latin, in French, in German, some lines in Old Norse also, in Italian of course, since I have read and reread the *Divine Comedy* half a dozen times. My memory is full of verses, but not full of dates or of place names. I forget those things. I forget the chronological order of things that happen to me. But somehow words cling to me or I cling to them.

AUDIENCE: A book that you published in 1925, *Inquisiciones,* I read that you have tried to purchase old copies and burn them. Could you explain?

BORGES: I am sorry to say that's true. The book was quite a bad book. I was trying to be at the same time Leopoldo Lugones, Don Francisco de Quevedo, and Sir Thomas Browne, and I failed of course. That book will disappear, I hope.

BARNSTONE: What about your first book of poems?

BORGES: My first book of poems, *Fervor de Buenos Aires,* came out in 1923. It was really my fourth book. I destroyed three books before publishing that one. Then I asked my father, who was a learned man, to go over it, and he said no, you must make and unmake your own mistakes. And when he died I found a copy of the book. The book was full of emendations, whole poems were rejected, and then I used that edition emended by my father for what is called *Obras completas, The Complete Works of Borges.* I owe that to my father. He never showed me the book, he never said a word about it, but I knew how he felt since I have seen that copy, that copy greatly emended, and greatly emended for the better, by my father.

BARNSTONE: Is it true that you put copies of the book in the raincoat pockets of critics in public places and then when you changed your mind you tried to get the books back from the bookstores?

BORGES: Yes, that is a true story. It is so unlikely that it is true. The thing actually happened.

AUDIENCE: You state that literature has inspired you, in your own literature—

BORGES: My own literature, no, I should say literature of other men. But I think that the books are inspiring. The reading of a book is an experience, like the experience, let us say, of looking at a woman, falling in love, walking across the street. Reading is an experience, a very real experience.

AUDIENCE: My question is really to find out if other arts inspire you, because I am curious to know the genesis of *Para las seis cuerdas.* *

BORGES: I dislike the tango and I like the *milonga,* and so I wrote lyrics for *milongas,* and I have tried to avoid local color since local color is false, and to avoid slang since slang comes and goes. I have used the elemental words of Spanish. I think it is quite a good book, *Para las seis cuerdas.* As to music, I can only tell you this. I work with Adolfo Bioy Casares, and his wife, Silvana Ocampo, puts records on the gramaphone, and we found out that certain records did us no good and that others

* *For Six Chords,* a book of poems for the *milonga* (a fast tango).

made for good. We found out that the records that did not inspire us came from Debussy, and the records that inspired us came from Brahms, and so we stuck to Brahms.

AUDIENCE: What do you feel about Argentina and the Argentine people? Do you seem to be able to understand why Argentina is the way it is today?

BORGES: I think that the Argentine Republic is as mysterious as the universe. I don't understand it.

9

I Always Thought of
Paradise As a Library

New York PEN Club,
March 1980

I knew that my destiny would be to read,
to dream, well, perhaps to write, but that
was not essential. And I always thought of
paradise as a library, not as a garden.

We also have been created by Edgar Allan
Poe, that splendid dreamer, that sad dreamer,
that tragic dreamer.

ALASTAIR REID: You once said in London—and I was sitting beside
you on the occasion in 1970—that all great literature eventually became
children's literature and you hoped in the long run your work would
be read by children. Would you like to amplify that?

JORGE LUIS BORGES: Yes. I think that that statement is true, though
I said it. For example, the works of Edgar Allan Poe are read by children.
I read them when I was a child. The *Arabian Nights* are read by children.
But maybe that's all to the good, since, after all, children read as we
should read. They are simply enjoying what they read. And that is the
only kind of reading that I permit. One should think of reading as a form
of happiness, as a form of joy, and I think that compulsory reading is
wrong. You might as well talk of compulsory love or compulsory happiness. One should be reading for the pleasure of the book. I was a teacher
of English literature for some twenty years and I always said to my
students: if a book bores you, lay it aside. It hasn't been written for you.
But if you read and feel passion, then go on reading. Compulsory reading
is a superstition.

JOHN COLEMAN: Borges, I've always had the impression that you
instinctively sympathized with Henry James' characterization of the
Russian novel as a loose, baggy monster, and I wonder if you still agree

with such general descriptions, grosso modo, of the Russian novel and of the novel in general as a genre.

BORGES: I have read but few novels in my life, but I don't like to say anything against the novel since then I would be sinning against Conrad and Stevenson, of course, and Dostoyevsky, and the second part of *Don Quixote,* so that maybe I was wrong when I wrote against the novel.

COLEMAN: I was told that when one of your early books, *Ficciones,* arrived here in New York, it was rejected on the grounds that the reader for the house here in New York said that these stories by Mr. Borges are very fine but why don't we wait for a big novel?

BORGES: I am not a reader of novels so I can hardly be a writer of novels, because all novels, even the finest novels, always include padding, while a short story can be essential all the time. For example, the last stories that Rudyard Kipling wrote or the last stories of Henry James or the tales of Conrad—those are essential. Why not the tales of the *Arabian Nights?* There is no padding to be found there. But in general a novel seems to me, to a writer at least, a weariness of the flesh.

REID: We thought we would ask you, Borges, about all the things we didn't understand in your work.

BORGES: I wonder if I understand them myself. I wager I don't.

REID: John and I decided that we would ask you about two or three words that quiver in your work, and the one word—

BORGES: Yes, I know, the word *labyrinth,* thank you.

REID: No, no, no.

BORGES: Thank you. It's a word like it.

REID: It's a little more mysterious than labyrinth. It's the word *asombro* that you use in your writing, and the expression *horror sagrado.* These are words that seem to me absolutely fundamental to your work. Would you tell us what you mean by *asombro?*

BORGES: By *asombro* I suppose I mean what I am feeling all the time. I am *astonished* by things, I'm taken aback by things. That's what I mean, and as to the other, the *horror sagrado,* you can find it in one of the finest poems in the English language:

> Weave a circle round him thrice
> And close your eyes with holy dread,
> For he on honey-dew hath fed,
> And drunk the milk of Paradise.*

*Samuel Taylor Coleridge, "Kubla Khan," lines 51–54.

What a fine line the last one is. "And drunk the milk of Paradise." You think of that milk as being terrible, as being awestriking, as being uncanny. "Weave a circle round him thrice/ And close your eyes with holy dread." That would be the sacred horror.

REID: In other words, is *horror sagrado* a translation of "holy dread" of Coleridge?

BORGES: I think that "holy dread" should be a translation of something from Latin, of what the Romans felt. I remember reading somewhere, I think in Pater's *Marius the Epicurean,* that there were certain places that the Romans regarded as holy and that the Romans would say about them *numen in est* "there is a god inside," there is something divine about it. So it had to be *horror sagrado. Horror divino* "divine horror," which is the same thing, has also been used by Góngora.

REID: But *asombro* is a feeling you often attribute to quite innocuous objects in the house.

BORGES: Perhaps the virtue of that word for you lies in the fact that when you say *asombro* you think of *sombra,* you think of shadow just as when you say *amazement* you think of a maze. But with *asombro* you think of shadow and of something at the same time unknowable.

COLEMAN: Borges, I was going to ask you about a word that is in one of the autobiographical short stories, "The South." When you talk about the discord in your genealogy between your mother's and your father's side, of a military and courageous man and a man of letters, and you talk about Juan Dahlmann, who may or may not be you, and you talk about—

BORGES: Well, I think he was. It's strictly confidential, I think he was. Don't say a word, eh?

COLEMAN: So could you talk about *discordia* and this wonderful sense you have of being a man split between your two genealogies?

BORGES: Maybe I was divided. I don't think of it as discord today. There are main strains. I think of my English forefathers, of my Portuguese forefathers, of my Spanish forefathers, of my Jewish forefathers, and I think they agree, that they are essentially friendly. But of course they stand for a different thing. Since of my Argentine and Uruguayan background I think of many military men, and then of my English background I think of Methodist preachers, of doctors of philosophy, and I think of books chiefly. But in the case of my mother's side, I think of swords, of battles, not of books. But after eighty years of living, the discord has been softened. I don't think of it as discord but rather a form of diversity. I may be enriched by those strains.

COLEMAN: So in the end you sense no discord.

BORGES: No, I am grateful.

COLEMAN: I was wondering if I could try your patience once more. It is the word *sueño,* which is an impossible word to translate because in English it means both *sleep* and *a dream.*

BORGES: No, not in English. No, in Spanish you mean.

COLEMAN: Excuse me, thank you.

BORGES: In English we have the two words, *dream* and *sleep.* In Spanish we have merely *sueño.* We must put up with it.

COLEMAN: Could you talk a bit about what the word *sueño* means in your own work?

BORGES: I suppose it depends on the context. It may mean *un sueño* "a dream" or *sueño* "sleep." I know nothing about that—that's Spanish grammar.

REID: Are you always sure yourself which of the two you mean when you use the word *sueño?*

BORGES: Well, I suppose I go in for ambiguities as all poets do. In that case I am enriched by that particular poverty of the Spanish language.

REID: I have one question which is very fundamental to—

BORGES: Only one?

REID: For the time being. One at a time.

BORGES: Yes, one at a time. And the night is young.

REID: And it begins—

BORGES: And the night is always young!

REID: Again, it begins with the phrase you once said, really crucially: "I don't write fiction. I invent fact."

BORGES: I think that sentence is a gift from you and I thank you.

REID: Shall we suppose for a moment that you once said that?

BORGES: It's good if I did.

REID: Yes, I think it's very likely that you did.

BORGES: Who knows? I may be guilty of that sentence.

REID: Guilty?

BORGES: Well, not guilty, but I wonder if I can live up to that sentence.

REID: What would you say is the difference? I don't write fiction. I invent fact.

BORGES: I suppose there is no difference between fact and fiction.

REID: This is a fairly radical point of view to express this evening.

BORGES: Well, solipsism or the past, what is the past but all memory? What is the past but memories that have become myth?

REID: But at the same time you have often obfuscated fiction by pretending that it's fact. As the people who look up the references in your stories know to their costs: two of them are true and the third they can't find anywhere. Now, have you done that deliberately? You have been playing—

BORGES: Yes, I did that deliberately when I was young. Now I am too old for those games. I want to tell simple, straightforward tales. I don't go in for literary hoaxes. All that happened a long time ago, to somebody else, to somebody else who wrote "Pierre Menard" and called it *Don Quixote*.

REID: The habit has been less easy to shed than you pretend. I think you still play around deliberately with ambiguities we all feel between fact and fiction. I mean, are we sure what is the difference?

BORGES: We are not sure about anything. Why should we be sure about these particular points? We live in such a mysterious universe. Everything is a riddle.

REID: It may be mysterious enough without some people making it more mysterious than it appears to be.

BORGES: Of course I don't really believe in free will. I have to play in that game. Playing that game and others is my destiny. I think of my destiny as being a literary destiny. Ever since I was a child I knew that would be my destiny. When I read biographies of Coleridge and De Quincey, of Milton also, they all knew that their destiny would be literary. And I knew that from the beginning. I knew that my destiny would be to read, to dream, well, perhaps to write, but that was not essential. And I always thought of paradise as a library, not as a garden. (You find that line in one of my poems.) That means that I was always dreaming.

REID: You mean that's a line from *Poema de los dones,* "Poem of the Gifts."

BORGES: Yes, that's it.

REID: You think of paradise as a library?

BORGES: And when I attained that library I was blind.

REID: That's the irony of that poem.

BORGES: Not the irony of that poem but "God's irony." "God's irony."*

COLEMAN: May I ask you about genres? You have practiced so many genres. You are an all-round literary man. Poems, essays, and stories.

*"God's irony" is a phrase from "Poem of the Gifts."

BORGES: "All-round literary man." That's from Stevenson.

COLEMAN: And I was wondering—

BORGES: I love him. Go ahead.

COLEMAN: Could you tell us why you love the work of Robert Louis Stevenson? It's more than *Treasure Island* for you. Can you say why?

BORGES: I don't think Stevenson has to be explained. If you don't sense Stevenson, then there is something wrong about you. I remember a line out of Angelus Silesius. I am translating his work with María Kodama. Angelus Silesius, the seventeenth-century German mystic wrote: *Die Ros' ist ohn' warum,/ sie blühet weil sie blühet,* "The rose has no why,/ she blooms as she blooms." I suppose that Stevenson has no why either. Besides, why explain Stevenson? It's enough for me to recall some lines of his. And then no explanation is needed:

> Under the wide and starry sky,
> Dig the grave and let me lie.
> Glad did I live and gladly die,
> And I laid me down with a will.*

Well, that's sufficient. If that doesn't explain Stevenson to you, then nothing will. One of his best books is more or less unknown because he wrote it in collaboration with his stepson—the novel *The Wrecker*. And another work of his I greatly like is *The Ebb Tide*. He wrote that also in collaboration with Lloyd Osbourne.

COLEMAN: It just occurred to me that many of your friends here might not also know of your intense admiration and love for Mark Twain.

BORGES: The explanation is very simple. I have read *Huckleberry Finn.* And that should be sufficient, more than sufficient.

COLEMAN: But could you speak of how North American literature has affected your own life as a writer?

BORGES: I think that North American literature has affected the whole world, affected all literature. Literature would not be what it is today had it not been for two men, Edgar Allan Poe and Walt Whitman. And you can add Mark Twain, Emerson, Thoreau, Melville, Emily Dickinson, Hawthorne, and you can go on and on, and not least is Robert Frost. It has affected the whole world, or at least the whole literary one. You can't think them away. They stand up still.

COLEMAN: But what you say is manifestly untrue as it applies to

---

*"Requiem," lines 1–4.

Spanish literature and to Spanish-American literature. It hasn't had that much effect upon—

BORGES: It has. I venture to disagree with you. You can't think of *modernismo* without Hugo, Verlaine, and not least Edgar Allan Poe. And Edgar Allan Poe came to us through France, although we are fellow Americans. I think Edgar Allan Poe cannot be thought away or argued away. You may like or dislike what he wrote, but his influence cannot be denied. He begat Baudelaire, who begat Mallarmé, and so on.

COLEMAN: Everyone knows that you love detective stories . . .

BORGES: Well, the genre was invented by Poe. He created the whole thing. He created a very strange character: the reader of detective stories. We also have been created by Edgar Allan Poe, that splendid dreamer, that sad dreamer, that tragic dreamer.

COLEMAN: I started a question but thankfully I got a little off the track, but now I would like to go back to it . . .

BORGES: I'm off the track all the time. That's what you are here for.

COLEMAN: People always say that there is not much of a difference when you practice poem, essay, and story, it's one literature by Borges. My question is how the same impulse might result in a poem, or an essay or a story, or maybe all three.

BORGES: I sense a plot. I see the beginning and the end. That plot may be the plot of a poem or of a sonnet. I think there is no essential difference. The essential difference lies in the reader, not in the writer. For example, if you see a page printed as prose, then you expect or fear information or argument. But if you see it printed as verse, then you expect, and maybe you get, emotion, passion, and so on. But I suppose they are essentially the same. Except that Stevenson thought the difference lay in the difficulty. There are many literatures that never attained prose. I don't think the Anglo-Saxons attained prose, although they wrote very powerful poetry. Poetry always comes, at least as far as my historical knowledge goes, before prose. Now, according to Stevenson, the reason is the fact that once you have achieved a unit, let's say a verse, then you merely have to repeat the pattern. That unit may be an alliterative verse as in the case of the Norsemen and of the Saxons, or it may be a rhymed verse, or it may be a question of long and short syllables, of hexameter. But once you have attained it then you merely have to repeat it. But in the case of prose it has to be changed all the time, and it has to be changed in such a way as to make it pleasant to the reader. That is far more difficult.

REID: If I may add to that, I have noticed in conversations with you over the years that you have infinitely more respect for poetry than you have for prose. You have a kind of imbued respect for poetry, as though it were something far superior to prose.

BORGES: I suppose you're right.

REID: Nevertheless, in your practice it strikes me you don't make much difference in what you bring off with prose and poetry.

BORGES: Personally I think that my poetry, such as it is, is better than my prose. But my friends tell me that I'm wrong. If they are poets they tell me I am an intruder in poetry. If they write prose fiction they tell me I'm an intruder. I don't know. Maybe—

REID: I think you've made a mockery of the difference between prose and poetry.

BORGES: Yes. I think there is no essential difference.

REID: I don't think so either.

BORGES: I think we are both right. We should be very happy.

REID: You always cite Stevenson, Chesterton, and Kipling, with occasional concessions to De Quincey and Sir Thomas Browne—

BORGES: No, no. Not occasionally I hope.

REID: Okay, okay.

BORGES: And Dr. Johnson, thank you.

REID: But the writer I think you are closest to in my mind is Coleridge.

BORGES: Coleridge, yes.

REID: Although you don't write much or talk much about Coleridge, Coleridge is the writer you are the reincarnation of, it would seem to me. Do you feel that too?

BORGES: I'm very thankful to you. I wish I were Coleridge. Yet Coleridge wrote but three poems, really. He wrote "Kubla Khan," he wrote "Cristabel," and "The Ancient Mariner." And "Ode to Dejection" and that's that. All the rest may safely be forgotten.

REID: But his prose also must have had a great effect on you.

BORGES: Yes, it has. But I wonder if Coleridge's prose had an effect on me or whether Coleridge first came to me through De Quincey, who has much the same music. I think really that when I admire De Quincey and enjoy him I am really admiring Coleridge.

REID: Translated.

BORGES: Yes, translated into very splendid nightmares.

COLEMAN: At the table we were talking about Dr. Johnson's letter to

McPherson, otherwise known as *Ossian*. And you felt quite strongly that the birth of European romanticism was to be found in a Scotsman, in an imposter.

BORGES: I don't think he was an imposter. I think he was a great poet, but he wanted his poem to belong to his country, not to himself. So he was really a great poet and a very important poet. I think that the romantic movement, the whole thing, began, I'm glad to say, in Scotland in the eighteenth century.

REID: I wish I could agree with you.

BORGES: You're not too sure.

REID: I'm not too sure.

COLEMAN: Why do you think that Johnson fulminated against McPherson to the extent he did in the letter?

BORGES: I venture to think that the real reason is that Johnson felt that his whole style, that his whole religion of poetry, was threatened by something new. He must have felt the presence of *Ossian* as a threat, even as Tennyson thought of Walt Whitman as a threat—something quite new, something quite different, something not altogether understandable, had occurred and they both felt threatened. I remember somebody asked Tennyson: "What do you think of Walt Whitman?" And Tennyson answered: "I am aware of Walt Whitman. I think of him as a wade in the ocean. No, sir, I don't think about Walt Whitman." Because he knew that he could not afford to do so. They are too dangerous. I think the remark of Johnson came out of fear, and that remark of Tennyson also. He knew something was happening and then the whole structure would tumble down.

COLEMAN: I get the sense that you're not threatened by any author.

BORGES: No, I try to think of all authors as friends. Sometimes I failed. Sometimes I'm defeated. But I go on. I try to enjoy every single book I read. I do my best to agree with it.

COLEMAN: In 1924–25 you published a book of essays called *Inquisiciones*.

BORGES: An awful book, yes.

REID: Ah. But wait a minute now.

BORGES: Why remember it?

REID: But I must plow on for a moment now. Permit me a few seconds.

BORGES: The one thing I remember is that it was quite bad and the binding was green.

REID: But there were those essays on Quevedo and Unamuno and Sir Thomas Browne. Now this is a book that you have prohibited and forbidden from being republished.

BORGES: Some ideas are good but the writing is bad. I don't say a word against Unamuno or Hugo or Sir Thomas Browne. But what I wrote about them is bosh, sheer bosh.

COLEMAN: So you believe in burying books that you would like to forget? And not have them republished under any circumstances?

BORGES: The real reason for a publication of *Obras completas, The Complete Works,* is that two books should be left out. *Inquisiciones* and another *cuyo nombre no quiero acordarme.** That was the real reason, the omission of those two books.

COLEMAN: That was the question. I was trying to elicit from you some dithyrambs against those books to figure out why they weren't in *The Complete Works.*

BORGES: Well, they were written in an absurd style, in a baroque style. I was baroque when I was a young man. I did my best to be Sir Thomas Browne, to be Lugones, to be Quevedo, to be somebody else. But now I'm content with my own humble self, if it exists, my private self, if the private self is to be found.

COLEMAN: If you started as a baroque writer, how did you become classic?

BORGES: I started as a baroque writer, as all young men do, out of timidity. A young man thinks: I write such and such a thing. But then he thinks, well, this is trivial. I have to disguise it. And he disguises it by being baroque. A form of shyness, really. Aggressive shyness, perhaps.

COLEMAN: So you became more daring and became plainer.

BORGES: Yes, now I am daring and I write in a straightforward way and use no word to send a reader to the dictionary, and avoid violent metaphors.

REID: We have decided to ask you a practical question.

BORGES: I wonder if I can answer a practical question. I'm not a practical man.

REID: It is very curious to me that—for instance, this most recent phase of your life—you have begun to travel more and more and more and more, whereas most people think of this period of their life as one in which they stay at home.

*"Whose name I do not wish to remember," allusion to the first line of *Don Quixote: En un lugar de la Mancha cuyo nombre no quiero acordarme.*

BORGES: If I stay at home I am repeating the same day over and over again. When I travel every day is different. Every day brings a gift. So I enjoy traveling, and so on. But if I stay home the whole thing is rather drab. Every day is the mirror of the day that came before it.

REID: I remember that you once said to me in Buenos Aires that newspapers are headed for oblivion. That's why they have to come out every day.

BORGES: They are meant for oblivion, while books . . .

REID: That's right, books are aiming higher.

BORGES: They strive to be everlasting. Some of them that last aren't.

REID: In speaking of other writers you have mentioned almost exclusively English and American writers, at least so far. Is this only because you were addressing an English audience? Do you consider yourself to be an "English" writer? Or does the question of nationality not enter into your writing? Would you respond to the place of nationality in literature, or in your own writing?

BORGES: I am not interested in nationality. It is a superstition.

REID: You think it is a superstition?

BORGES: As to English literature, I think it is *the* literature. But I don't say that against other literatures. At the same time I greatly love the German language and German literature, and I love French literature and I dislike the French language. But of course I must broaden it to *all* English literature. If I think of the Bible, I think of the King James Bible. When I think of the *Arabian Nights,* I think of the *Arabian Nights* in terms of Lane and Burton.

REID: And was it in fact true that you read *Don Quixote* in English before you read it in Spanish?

BORGES: No. You can quote that, why not?

REID: It's a very useful metaphor. You always spoke to me of that edition of the English translation that you have that you read.

BORGES: No, I think I was speaking of Dante's *Divine Comedy,* as done into English by Longfellow. I began reading the *Divine Comedy* in English.

COLEMAN: Borges, you have spoken of literary men you admire, what about literary women? Could you identify the women in literature whose contribution you consider most significant?

BORGES: I think I would limit myself to one, to Emily Dickinson.

COLEMAN: Is that it?

BORGES: That's that. Short and sweet.

REID: I think it should be pointed out, however, that there are more.

BORGES: Yes of course. There is Silvina Ocampo, for example, who is translating Emily Dickinson at this moment in Buenos Aires.

REID: Changing the note, the question here comes quite bluntly, and I feel no reason not to deliver it just as bluntly. Speak to us about death. You don't feel threatened by any writer. Do you feel threatened by death?

BORGES: I think of death as being full of hope. Hope of annihilation. Hope of being forgotten. Sometimes I feel unhappy. I can't help it. Then I say: But after all why should I be unhappy, since at any moment I may die? And that comes to me as a comfort. Because I think of death as being total. I don't want to go on. I've lived far too long. Why go on after death? That's an exaggeration. I stand in hope of death, not in fear of death.

COLEMAN: How would you have written differently had you written in English?

BORGES: I respect the English language too much. I have done most of my reading in English. I wonder if it would have been greatly different.

COLEMAN: You said once—I'm sorry to repeat a sentence which you may not want to have repeated—but you did say: "I would have liked to have been born an Englishman." I remember your saying that.

BORGES: But in a sense I was born to English, since at home I spoke English and Spanish. So that I was born to English. Though my oral English may not be really effective, my reader's English is quite good.

COLEMAN: Maybe the question is too blunt, and I was wondering if I might tease it out a bit. Do you feel that your own prose style, which is unique in Spanish—

BORGES: But is it, really?

COLEMAN: Yes.

BORGES: I wonder.

COLEMAN: Some writers who are so-called bilingual writers say: "Sometimes I think in one language and then I put it into another language."

BORGES: I'm doing that all the time with Latin. People have been trying to write Latin in different languages. For example, Sir Thomas Browne, for example, Quevedo, were all writing Latin in English or in Spanish.

REID: I would like to make a little hiatus here and ask you to tell us that story about the *taxista* in Chicago and what he said to you the other day.

BORGES: The taxi driver.

REID: The taxi driver, yes.

BORGES: That was the day before yesterday, or yesterday, I'm not sure. My days are very hazy. He had been a soldier. He had known bitterness. He had known unhappiness. Then he suddenly said without realizing the full power of his spoken word. He suddenly said: "I hate memory." I thought that very fine, and I think I'll grab that and use it. I'll annex that sentence "I hate memory." It's a beautiful sentence. Flee and forget the world.

COLEMAN: You once said that you would like to discover yourself a Jew. Why?

BORGES: I suppose I am partly a Jew. Not through the fact that my forefathers were called Acevedo or Pinedo, but merely by the fact that one of the fundamental books, or the essential books, is the Bible, and I was brought up on the Bible. I should say that all of us—and it has nothing to do with genealogy, with blood—we are all of us in the West Greeks and Hebrews. Those are the two essential nations, Greece and Israel. After all, Rome is but an extension of Greece.

COLEMAN: Borges, people read to you now. When you read a book you hear it. Most of the books, it seems to me, that you talk about are books that you read when you were a child in that paradise of your father's library.

BORGES: I'm always rereading rather than reading.

COLEMAN: Are you rereading in your memory what you read or are people reading to you again?

BORGES: Both things, I should say. My memory is full of quotations, as you know only too well. But also, kind friends come and we take a book, generally by Conrad, by Stevenson, by Kipling, and we read on.

COLEMAN: As an example of this, I was told that Graham Greene went to see you in Buenos Aires. Graham Greene said to you, well, about Stevenson's poetry . . .

BORGES: I don't think he went to see me. He's far too important a person to do that. I think I went to see him.

COLEMAN: Let us assume that you were the aggressor in this case. But Greene recounts that you were talking about Stevenson, and Greene said to you that Stevenson wrote one great poem, and Greene didn't name the poem, but then you recited it.

BORGES: I suppose it was "Requiem." I'm not sure. It may have been "Ticonderoga," he wrote so many fine poems, and every single one of them is the best poem he wrote. He achieved perfection.

REID: Do you see a meld of languages, for instance, Anglo-Hispanic, as a possibility in the future?

BORGES: No, let us hope not. I hope that both will survive in their purity. I don't think anything of it.

REID: I've just come back from Puerto Rico yesterday and I can testify that such a meld is in progress there. But they wouldn't enrich one another, necessarily. They would only intrude on one another, as they do in fact. Do you notice when you are changing languages? For instance, at dinner tonight you were changing several times and I don't think you realized.

BORGES: No. I never realized it. I was shifting from one to the other.

REID: All the time.

BORGES: Yes. I was at home in both of them.

REID: What fascinated me about Emir Rodríguez Monegal's biography, which you haven't read, of course—

BORGES: No, I haven't read it. The subject hardly interests me.

REID: Yes, the subject hardly interests you—was that English was associated very much with your father and Spanish with your mother.

BORGES: That's true. My father always spoke to me in English.

REID: He did, really?

BORGES: When my father died—that happened in 1938—my mother began to study English in order to be near him.

REID: I see.

BORGES: Then she made translations from the English of books by Sir Herbert Reed, by Saroyan.

REID: She translated on her own.

BORGES: On her own, yes. She did books by Virginia Woolf and others.

REID: But you had a certain distinction between English and Spanish in the sense that you said that English was the language of the library and that Spanish was the language of the household, of the practical household.

BORGES: I suppose it was. I think of English as being a very physical language, far more physical than Spanish, as in such phrases as "pick yourself up."

REID: Did your father never speak to you in Spanish?

BORGES: Oh yes, he did. Of course he used both languages. But I knew that I had to speak in a certain way to one of my grandmothers, and in a different way to the other one. And then I found out those two ways were called the Spanish language and the English language. That was natural.

REID: So you just thought of it as different manners of address, as it were, for a while.

BORGE: Different ways of talking to two different persons.

REID: So that languages are associated with people more than with things in themselves.

BORGES: Yes, a child doesn't know what language he is speaking. If you tell a child he's speaking Chinese, he believes you.

REID: He doesn't need to know.

BORGES: No. The things are given him.

REID: So you don't see any glowing future for "Spanglish" as it's called.

BORGES: No!

COLEMAN: Borges, your father wrote a novel, which very few people have read. Could you tell us something about that novel, which was published, I think, in Majorca. Is that true?

BORGES: It was published in Majorca, as far as I remember. He told me to rewrite it, and he gave me a set of chapters as they should be rewritten. And I intend to do that. The novel is a good one.

COLEMAN: Why don't you rewrite that book now? Might that be one of your ambitions?

BORGES: I will be rewriting that book within ten days or so. I can't do it here in the States.

COLEMAN: Could you tell us something about the novel? Do you remember it at all? Because your father was a father who always wanted *you* to be a writer. No one would characterize him as a writer as such. He was a man of letters, but . . .

BORGES: He wrote some very fine sonnets. He also wrote a book of Easter short stories. He also wrote a drama, a book of essays. And he destroyed them. As for the novel, if you wait a year or so you will know all about it. I can't tell you the plot.

COLEMAN: You mean you are going to rewrite the novel.

BORGES: Yes, I am going to rewrite it the way he wanted it to be rewritten. Not the way I would do the job myself. I want to save that book, an historical novel, about the civil war in our country in the nineteenth century.

COLEMAN: Most children are not brought up instructed to be writers from the very moment that they are born.

BORGES: But I wonder whether I *was* instructed. I think that I *felt* that.

COLEMAN: You felt it.

BORGES: Yes.

REID: It's described as a tacit understanding.

BORGES: Yes, a tacit understanding, yes. That's the right word.

REID: Nobody was responsible.

BORGES: Yes, it was a part of the universe, a part of destiny.

REID: Which you accepted as an inevitability.

BORGES: Yes, but at the same time, I was thankful.

REID: Were you intimidated by the realization that your destiny was to be a writer?

BORGES: On the contrary, I was very happy about it. My father said: "Read as much as you can. Write when you have to do it, and, above all, don't rush into print."

REID: Borges told once an amazing story about his first book.

BORGES: The one in Buenos Aires.

REID: No, the one before that sold seventy-five copies.

BORGES: As many as seventy-five, I wonder. You are exaggerating a bit.

REID: Borges said that since his first book sold seventy-five copies, he felt that it was still within his control because he could physically visit all the people who had bought a copy and apologize and ask for it back and promise that the next book would be better. But when his second book sold seven hundred and fifty copies, he said that the public was already an abstraction, and the work was out of his hands. What do you feel now when your books sell seventy-five thousand copies?

BORGES: I think I am ringed in by very generous people. They're wrong of course, but what can I do about it?

REID: Borges, had it ever occurred to you sometimes that you use modesty somewhat like a club?

BORGES: I'm very sorry. I apologize. I'm not using modesty, I'm being sincere.

REID: That's just an observation, Borges, please forgive *me*.

BORGES: No! We're all together.

REID: However, to substantiate the rudeness of my remark, I must—

BORGES: No!

REID: I must tell a story. When I met you once in Scotland we were driving back and you asked me what I'd been doing recently and I said that I had written some poems. Then you thought for a minute and you said: "I too have written some verses."

BORGES: Some lines, yes, not verses.

REID: Some lines, that's right. Modesty carried to an extreme that I found a little . . .

BORGES: Embarrassing.

REID: A little embarrassing.

BORGES: I'm sorry. I apologize.

REID: You have on more than one occasion alluded to surrealism as producing an art and literature of no value or interest. You have even compared it unfavorably with expressionism.

BORGES: But of course.

REID: Would you please explain and develop this view?

BORGES: I think there is a wide difference. The expressionists were mystics, for example, while the surrealists aimed at astonishing the readers. I think expressionism *was* important, in their painting also. Kandinsky, Marc Chagall, Beckman, they were poets. Then—of course this is my personal bias—I love German, and I rather tend to dislike French. Not French literature, of course, because I much admire it, but the French language. There is something petty about it. Something trivial about it. As a good Argentine, I shouldn't say those things. But really, that's the way I feel about it. Maybe it's my English background at work.

REID: Have you always found that some languages fit you better than others or suit you better than others?

BORGES: I wish I could achieve English or achieve German, or achieve Latin. I wonder if I have achieved Spanish, for that matter. Maybe I have made a muddle of the whole thing.

COLEMAN: May I ask Borges about expressionist film? And early film. Films that you remember seeing.

BORGES: I wonder if they were expressionist. I think of films by Joseph von Sternberg, for example, films like *Underworld, The Showdown, The Dragnet.* I remember I have seen those over and over again. And also Orson Welles' *Citizen Kane.* I've seen that several times over.

COLEMAN: I think you may have said on one occasion that you saw *West Side Story* seventeen times. Is that true?

BORGES: I must have seen it perhaps sixteen times, or three or four times. *Porgy and Bess* also.

COLEMAN: Could you tell us what appealed to you in a film by Sternberg or a film by Eisenstein. What was the technique that appealed to you that might possibly have some relation with your writing?

BORGES: I never thought much of Eisenstein whatever. I worship Joseph von Sternberg. I think he was a far better director. What I liked in Sternberg was the fact that he was laconic. That he would give you, let's say, a murder in three scenes, three images. I enjoyed something in his style that I see akin to Seneca.

COLEMAN: It was the laconic quality of the narration.

BORGES: Yes, it was. And I tried to ape that quality, I played the sedulous ape to Sternberg, when I wrote a too famous story called "The Streetcorner Man." I was doing my best to be Joseph von Sternberg, and to be Chesterton also.

COLEMAN: But what about other American films, the classic American films, Borges?

BORGES: I have always enjoyed the westerns. Especially *La hora señalada.*

COLEMAN: *High Noon?*

BORGES: Yes, *High Noon,* yes. It's a very fine film. There is something epic about it.

COLEMAN: How about Bogart films?

BORGES: I remember them, but in a rather dim way. I think chiefly of George Bancroft, or William Powell, of Fred Kohler, those actors who were gangsters, who played the part of gangsters.

COLEMAN: But why are there so many gangsters and evil people in your stories? You obviously love to see them in film, and there are certainly plenty of murderers in your stories. But you don't seem to be a very violent man.

BORGES: No, but I have known violent men. I am not a violent man of course.

COLEMAN: What do you mean when you say you've known violent men?

BORGES: Well, a friend of mine was a murderer. A very likable fellow.

COLEMAN: How about the Germanophiles of Buenos Aires?

BORGES: They are not interesting at all, so far as I remember.

COLEMAN: What sort of people were these people, these adorers of Hitler in 1941?

BORGES: They were nationalists. They were Catholics. I can't understand Catholicism or nationalism. Those things are unknown to me. I don't want to know anything about them. They are rather hateful to me. But why speak about it?

COLEMAN: Let's stop. We will stop.

REID: But just one more thing. Among the heroic figures throughout your writing are the *cuchilleros* "the knifers" in Buenos Aires, and you actually knew them. You talked to them, no?

BORGES: Yes, I did.

REID: The knife-fighters. Now that means that there was a stage for what we call "the law of the gun," or what we would call "the law of the knife" in Buenos Aires.

BORGES: Yes, but that was quite different because you had to be brave.

REID: And honorable, no?

BORGES: You can shoot a man at a distance. Knife-fighters? No. You had to challenge him. Then you had to choose your weapons and take your stand.

REID: So it was a duel, like fighting a duel.

BORGES: No, not a duel. For a duel you had to make an arrangement to fight.

REID: There were actual figures in your life, that you knew?

BORGES: At least one was. Why not mention the name of Don Nicolás Paredes in New York. He was my friend.

COLEMAN: Those *naipes de tahur* "gambler's cards."

BORGES: That rings a bell, eh, *tahur* is a fine word.

COLEMAN: It means gambler, is that right? There is a very prosaic question, and it is a question that is always asked of writers, but I hope you don't mind my asking it. The question is: What are your working methods? How do you work as a writer? You dictate.

BORGES: Yes, but I work all day and all night. All day I am scheming poems or fables. And at night I am dreaming and that's the same thing, going on. Then when people come I dictate maybe a stanza or a page to them.

COLEMAN: But, Borges, when you were writing out manuscripts, did you write out, let's say, a whole paragraph or did you inch ahead line by line? Do you recall how you composed?

BORGES: No, I began by the wrong method.

COLEMAN: Which is?

BORGES: The wrong method is to write a paragraph and emend it.

Then write a second paragraph. But that made the whole thing jolting all the time. But I think the real way is to write as much as you can and then to emend it. But not to revise one sentence and then begin the rough draft of another. You begin by making a rough draft of the whole thing.

REID: It's what's known among writers nowadays, Borges, as vomiting.

BORGES: Yes, that's right.

COLEMAN: No, *al fresco,* please. Italian.

BORGES: I would say retching. Anglo-Saxon.

10

The Nightmare, That
Tiger of the Dream

Indiana University,
April 1980

I am often haunted by nightmare.
And I feel that were I a theologian—happily
I am not—I might find an argument in
favor of hell. . . . The nightmare has a
peculiar horror to it. The nightmare, that
tiger of the dream.

WILLIS BARNSTONE: In the years that we have known each other
we have spoken almost exclusively about poetry.

JORGE LUIS BORGES: Yes. It's the only subject, really.

BARNSTONE: A few days ago when we took a plane in New York,
you asked what the name of the airline was, and I said TWA. You asked
what that stood for, and I said Trans World Airlines. Do you remember
what you said?

BORGES: Yes. I said that that stood for Walt Whitman Trans World.
He would have enjoyed that.

BARNSTONE: What about that pioneer transworld pilot?

BORGES: I think that what I have to say now is what I said quite some
time ago in an essay:* the fact, forgotten by many people, that Whitman
thought of *Leaves of Grass* as an epic, not as a series of short poems. Now,
the epic has been attempted many times, but there always was a central
figure. *Arma Virumque canō.* I mean you always had a character larger
than life. For example, you had Ulysses, you had Beowulf, you had
Roland. But when Walt Whitman thought of writing an epic, Sewuld he
thought, well, this should be an epic of democracy, and so I can't have a
central figure. In one of his poems he says: "There are painters who give
us pictures of crowds, and one of them has a halo. But I want all of my

* "Nota sobre Walt Whitman," "Note on Walt Whitman," *Discusión* (1932).

135

characters, all the people in my pictures, to have halos." And then he
came to a very strange scheme, and nobody seems to have remarked it,
since the people who imitated, or tried to imitate, Walt Whitman did
not imitate his method but the results of his method. I am thinking of
very important poets, for example, Carl Sandburg, Pablo Neruda, Edgar
Lee Masters. Since Whitman had to write an epic of democracy, he
created a character and that character is a very strange trinity, and yet
many people mistake him for the writer. But the writer is not the character. When Walt Whitman began, he thought of his own life. He
thought of having been born on Long Island, but he thought that this
isn't enough: I should have been born all over America. Then he created
that very strange character, Walt Whitman, not to be taken for the writer
of the book, the Brooklyn journalist, who had written a novel about
alcohol—he had written, I think, a tract in favor of slavery. But here he
attempted a very daring experiment, the most daring and the most successful experiment in all literature as far as I know. The experiment
was this. The central character would be called after the author, Walt
Whitman, but he was, firstly, Walt Whitman the human being, the very
unhappy man, who wrote *Leaves of Grass*. Then a magnification, or
transmogrification of that Walt Whitman, called Walt Whitman, who
was not the real Whitman at all, or at least not the Whitman his contemporaries knew, but a divine vagabond. And that man was a real character
in "Walt Whitman, a kosmos, of Manhattan the son,/ Turbulent, fleshy,
sensual, eating, drinking and breeding."* It appears from the biographies
that those facts are not quite true. We find many distressing things about
Whitman, but not about Walt Whitman. And then, since that character
had to be a trinity—for he thought of it as a trinity—he introduced a
third person. That third person is the reader.

So Walt Whitman is compounded of Walt Whitman the man, of
Walt Whitman the myth, and also of the reader, because he thought of
the reader as being also the hero of the book, being also the central man
of the picture. So the reader speaks to Walt Whitman, and asks him:
"What do you see, Walt Whitman? What do you hear, Walt Whitman?"
And then Whitman answers back, "I hear America" or, for example—
I'm an Argentine and I have chosen this particular example:

---

* "Song of Myself," 24, lines 497–98.

> I see the gaucho crossing the plains, I see the incomparable
>   rider of horses with his lasso on his arm,
> I see over the pampas the pursuit of wild cattle for their hides.*

"The incomparable rider of horses." That is taken of course from the last line of the *Iliad:* "Hector, tamer of horses." But had Whitman written "the incomparable rider," he would have written nothing, but "rider of horses" gives it that peculiar strength.

And so we have this very strange character: the Whitman whose dates are given in the dictionaries and is forgotten, the Whitman who died in Camden, the magnification of Whitman, and then the reader. And the reader is made to stand for all future readers, and he thought of them as being all Americans. He did not know that he would be known the world over. He never thought in terms of that. He thought in terms of America, and of America the democracy.

Sometimes Whitman tells things of himself. But since he wanted to be everybody, he said something that no poet had ever said. I think the verses go thus:

> These are really the thoughts of all men in all ages and lands,
>   they are not original with me,
> If they are not yours as much as mine they are nothing,
>   or next to nothing,
> If they are not the riddle and the untying of the riddle
>   they are nothing,
> If they are not just as close as they are distant
>   they are nothing.
> This is the grass that grows wherever the land is
>   and the water is,
> This common air that bathes the globe.†

Other poets, for example, Edgar Allan Poe or one of his disciples, Baudelaire, were trying to say uncommon things. They were trying to surprise the reader. Poets still keep on working at that game. But Whitman went further. Whitman thought of his thought as being the "thoughts of all men in all ages and lands." "They are not original with me." He wanted to be everybody else. He wanted to be all men. He even saw

---

*"Salut Au Monde," lines 122–23. In Whitman's version "gaucho" is "Wacho," a member of a Caddoan Indian Tribe, Texas.
†"Song of Myself," 17, lines 355–60.

himself as a pantheist, but the world is rather priggish. I think it comes from a deep feeling in Whitman. Now I wonder if that has been detected, because people read, and they don't think that they are one of the persons in that trinity which is Walt Whitman. And yet that was Whitman's idea. He wanted to stand for all America. In one of his poems, he writes:

> Now I tell what I knew in Texas in my early youth,
> (I will tell not the fall of Alamo,
> Not one escaped to tell the fall of Alamo,
> The hundred and fifty are dumb yet at Alamo,) *

Well, he never was in Texas in his life. And he also wrote: "As I have walk'd in Alabama my morning walk."† He never went to Alabama, as far as I know. But in another poem he says that he remembers having been born in the South. Of course I don't think he was born in several places at once, a kind of miracle. But still that made him into a great poet. Nobody seems to have attempted anything like it. They have just copied his intonation, his use of Biblical free verse, but nobody seems to have seen how strange was his personal experiment.

And even Walt Whitman did not live up to that one epic, because afterwards, there came the Civil War, and Walt Whitman was not all Americans. He was a partisan, as may be expected, on the side of the North. He did not think of himself as being also Southern, as he had felt himself in the beginning. And then in a sense he became less of Walt Whitman. He became someone in particular. He was no longer all men in all ages and lands. He was a contemporary of the War between the States. But should we say those things, since perhaps he wrote the most beautiful lines at the end of the book, when he says "Camerado"— he thought he was using Spanish but he was inventing the word:**

> Camerado, this is no book,
> Who touches this touches a man,
> (Is it night? are we here together alone?)
> It is I you hold and who holds you,
> I spring from the pages into your arms—decease calls me forth.‡

---

*"Song of Myself," 34, lines 871–74.
†"Starting from Paumanok," II, line 148.
**The Spanish word for "comrade" (masculine and feminine) is *camarada*.
‡"So Long!" lines 53–57.

And then:

> I am as one disembodied, triumphant, dead."*

The book ends with that single word of one syllable, *dead.* But the book is living. The book is still living, and every time that we open the book, every time that we go back to it (and I'm doing that all the time), we become part of that trinity. We are Walt Whitman. So I am grateful to Whitman, not for his ideas—after all, I have no personal use for democracy myself—but democracy was a tool needed by Whitman in order to form that extraordinary epic called *Leaves of Grass,* and changed from edition to edition. Emerson said that that book when it appeared was the "finest piece of wit and wisdom that America had yet contributed."

I think of Walt Whitman not only as a myth but as a friend of mine. I think of him as having been rather unhappy, and having worked himself into singing joy and happiness, and that has been done perhaps by another poet, perhaps in Spanish, by Jorge Guillén, who really gives us a sensation of happiness. And now and then Shakespeare. As for Whitman, you can always see that he was doing his best to be happy, although he really wasn't happy, and that is part of the interest he has for us. Well, now you should say something, I have been talking far too much, Barnstone.

BARNSTONE: One thing I wanted to ask you was—

BORGES: Why one thing, many things!

BARNSTONE: —what you think of Whitman's notion of writing one book all his life. And you mentioned Jorge Guillén as one who also wrote one book for at least thirty-one years, *Cántico.*†

BORGES: A very fine book.

BARNSTONE: The way Baudelaire also wrote one book, *Les Fleurs du Mal.*

BORGES: Yes, alas, he did.

BARNSTONE: What do you think of the notion of a writer, in the prophetic manner of Whitman, who dedicates his life to the elaboration of one long book?

---

*"So long!" line 71.
†Guillén (b. 1893) later added two more books, *Clamor* and *Homenaje,* which he incorporated into one book, *Aire Nuestro* (1968).

BORGES: Personally, I suppose all writers are writing the same book over and over again. But I suspect that every generation rewrites, with very slight variations, what the other generations wrote. I don't think a man can do much by himself since, after all, he has to use a language, and that language is a tradition. Of course he may change that tradition, but at the same time that tradition takes for granted all that came before it. I think Eliot said that we should try to renew with a minimum of novelty. And I remember that Bernard Shaw said, in a very unjust, derogatory way, of Eugene O'Neill: "There is nothing new about him except his novelties," meaning that novelties are trivial. As for one book —well, I wonder. All my writings have been bound together in a single volume. Maybe a few pages may survive.

BARNSTONE: It is very curious that Poe for Europe is what Whitman is for the Americas.

BORGES: Yes, and we owe that to France; we owe that to Baudelaire and to Mallarmé. When I was a boy, Poe was known to us through the French.

BARNSTONE: But why was Walt Whitman for the New World what Poe was for the Old World? Virtually every Latin American poet, including yourself, has a poem to Walt Whitman.

BORGES: I think that Whitman appealed to Europe also. I remember reading Whitman through a fine German translation by Johannes Schlaf. He also appeals to Europe. The fact is that America has given the world at least three names that cannot be thought away without changing everything. And those names are Whitman, the second one is Poe, and as to the last, I would choose Robert Frost. Other people might choose Emerson perhaps. You can do your own choosing. But America gave the world three men that cannot be thought away. They are essential. All contemporary literature would not be what it is had it not been for those two very different and those two very unhappy men, Edgar Allan Poe and Walt Whitman.

BARNSTONE: What specifically in the prosody of Whitman do you think the other writers imitated? Or if not prosody, what aspect of Whitman appealed to other writers?

BORGES: Of course Whitman was one of the many inventors of free verse, perhaps the most conspicuous. You read the psalms and you read Walt Whitman. You can see that of course he had read the psalms, but the music is different. Every poet evolves a music of his own, and almost a language of his own. After a great poet has passed through a language, then the language is no longer the same. Something has changed. And in the case of Walt Whitman, it did change. Now, Whitman went in for the vernacular. And at the same time, one feels that he did not know how to use it very well. And you find very ugly lines now and then. For example: "Americanos! conquerers! marches humanitarian!"* That is highly offensive, and he could write things like that. But those who mastered the vernacular used it after him. I mean two such diverse men as Mark Twain and Sandburg. They used the vernacular easily, while in the case of Walt Whitman, he rather floundered. He used French words, Spanish words, not too happily. At the same time I know that when I discovered Walt Whitman I was overwhelmed. I felt of him as the only poet. I had the same feeling afterwards with Kipling, I felt it with De Quincey, who wrote poetry in prose, and they were very different poets. But I thought of him at the time as being *the* poet, the man who had found the right way, the way in which poetry should be written. Of course there are many ways of writing poetry, all of them different from each other.

BARNSTONE: Would you be willing to comment on the poem you wrote about Whitman?

BORGES: Well, I don't recall the poem. Go ahead, I am very curious. Why don't you read it in the English translation where it will be greatly bettered? I know you will be very disappointed. That poem is no good.

BARNSTONE:

CAMDEN 1892

The smell of coffee and of newspapers.
Sunday and its boredom. It is morning.
Some allegorical verses are adorning
The skimmed over page: the vain pentameters
Of a happy colleague. The old man lies
Stretched out and white in his respectable
Poor man's room. Lazily he fills
The weary mirror with his gaze. His eyes
See a face. He thinks, now unsurprised: that face

* "Starting from Paumanok," 3, line 37.

Is me. With fumbling hand he reaches out
To touch the tangled beard and ravaged mouth.
The end is not far off. His voice declares:
I am almost gone, and yet my verses scan
Life and its splendor. I was Walt Whitman.*

BORGES: It's quite good, eh? Not too good but quite good, as far as it goes. That's the human Whitman only, not the myth.

BARNSTONE: Whitman thought of himself as a prophetic figure, writing a kind of Bible.

BORGES: Well, he did!

BARNSTONE: Frequently in your stories and poems, you don't write a Bible, but you aspire to secrets, to enigmas, to a single word.

BORGES: I am constantly being baffled by things.

BARNSTONE: You go different routes. Your work gets simpler and simpler, fewer and fewer words.

BORGES: Yes, I agree.

BARNSTONE: If Whitman could throw in an adjective, he did so.

BORGES: He did only too often, I should say.

BARNSTONE: His work might have been called *Broad Leaves of Grass,* because he usually added words to intensify, often not with the best results. What do you think of the fact that this poet, who is marvelous and uneven, manages—

BORGES: But he *is* marvelous and uneven. Silvina Ocampo said to me that a poet stood in need of bad verses. If not, the others would not stand out. We were commenting on Shakespeare. I said he has many bad verses. And she said: "That's all to the good. A poet should have bad verses." Only secondary poets write only good verses. Out of politeness you should have bad verses.

BARNSTONE: Eliot said there should be weaker words among the stronger ones so that the lines do not become crabbed. But among the hack works which you claim you have done was to translate a book of Walt Whitman's poetry. You say that Walt Whitman was your poet and meant so very much to you. What did he teach you?

BORGES: He taught me to be straightforward. That was the one lesson I learned from him. But teaching, after all, is not important. The fact is that I was overwhelmed by emotion, that I knew pages and pages of his

*Trans. Willis Barnstone.

work by heart, that I kept on saying them to myself in the day and in the night. I think that what's important is the way a man is moved when he reads poetry. If a man doesn't feel poetry physically, then he doesn't feel poetry at all. He had better become a professor or a critic. I think of poetry as being a very personal and a very important experience. Either you feel it or you don't. If you feel it, you don't have to explain it.

BARNSTONE: I am listening so intently that it wipes out further thoughts and questions. I stand in need of Edgar Allan Poe. Would you speak now about Poe?

BORGES: Every writer is undertaking two quite different works at the same time. One is the particular line he is writing, the particular story he is telling, the particular fable that came to him in a dream, and the other is the image he creates of himself. Perhaps the second task that goes on all throughout life is the most important. In the case of Poe, I think that our image of Poe is more important than any of the lines on the pages that he wrote. We think of Poe as we may think of a character in fiction. He is as vivid to us as Macbeth or Hamlet. And creating a very vivid image and leaving that to the memory of the world is a very important task. As to the verses of Edgar Allan Poe, I know some of them by heart, and I think them lovely, and others are not so good. For example, I will begin by verses I learned:

> Was it not Fate that, on this July midnight—
> Was it not Fate (whose name is also Sorrow)
> That bade me pause before the garden-gate,
> To breathe the incense of those slumbering roses?
> . . . .
> (Ah, bear in mind this garden was enchanted!)*

And also this very strange line from his first book, *Al Aaraaf*. I am not sure. My erudition is but dim:

> The eternal voice of God is passing by
> And the red winds are withering in the sky!†

And at the same time, when I think of the raven, I think of it as a stuffed

---

*"To Helen," lines 21–24, 30. This poem was written for Mrs. Sarah Helen Whitman.
†Lines 131–32.

raven. I cannot take it seriously! When the raven speaks, "Quoth the Raven 'Nevermore,' " that seems to me to be ineffective. Rossetti, who had read "The Raven" of course, did it better. He was inspired by Poe, but he wrote thus:

> Look in my face; my name is Might-have-been;
> I am also called No-More, Too-late, Farewell. . . . *

There is also that wonderful word invented by Bishop Wilkins in the seventeenth century, a word so fine that no poet has ever dared to use it. He invented two words. One, *everness*, and I was bold enough to use that as the title for a sonnet of mine, "Everness." Because *everness* is better than *eternity*. It goes with the German *Ewigkeit*. Then another word like *doom*, a word far better than that line I like so much in Dante: *Lasciate ogni speranza voi ch'entrate* "Abandon all hope you who enter here." That single word invented, given to the English language by Bishop Wilkins and never used because all those poets have stood in fear of it, that terrible, that beautiful, word is *neverness*. That could be done into German perhaps as *Nimmerkeit*. It can't be done into Spanish, I know. You see, *everness* is a fine word and *neverness* is a desperate word. Edgar Allan Poe wrote many verses and I don't think much of them, but there is one story of his that stands out, and that story is "The Narrative of Arthur Gordon Pym." You have Arthur and Edgar, both Saxon names, then Gordon and Allan, both Scottish. Then Pym goes for Poe. Now the first chapters of that long tale are not too memorable, I should say. But the last chapters are a nightmare. And they are, strangely enough, a nightmare of whiteness, of white being thought of as being terrible. Of course Herman Melville had read "The Narrative of Arthur Gordon Pym," and he wrote *Moby Dick, or the White Whale*. There he used the same idea, the idea of white, not scarlet or black, as being the most terrible of colors. You find that both books, *Moby Dick* and "The Narrative of Arthur Gordon Pym," are a nightmare of whiteness.

And of course Edgar Allan Poe created a genre. He created a detective genre. It seems to me that everything that has been done afterwards, all those things had already been thought out by Poe. You remember "The Mystery of Marie Rogêt," "The Murders of Rue Morgue," "The

---

*Sonnet 97, "A Superscription," from *The House of Life*.

Purloined Letter," and "The Gold Bug." Then you have all those many fine books that came afterwards. After all, Sherlock Holmes and Watson are but Poe and his friend, the Chevalier Auguste Dupin. Poe thought of many things. He thought that detective novels were artificial, so he did not seek a close reality. He placed them in France. His detective is a French detective, because he knew that it would be easier to deal with Paris— I don't think he knew Paris—the French—though he hardly knew them— than to write stories about contemporary happenings in New York. He was quite aware that detective fiction is a form of fantastic fiction. He invented all the conventions. He also invented something else. He invented the *reader* of the detective story. That is to say, when we read any detective story, when we read, for example, Eden Phillpotts, or Ellery Queen, or Nicholas Blake, we are really created by Edgar Allan Poe. He created a new type of reader. That of course has made for thousands of books all over the world. I have attempted the genre myself, writing detective stories, but I knew all the time that real writer was Edgar Allan Poe. So he has given us many things. He also gave us an idea, which I think is mistaken, but is very interesting: the idea that poetry can be made through reasoning. I suppose you remember what he wrote about "The Raven." He said that when he began he needed a word with an *o* and an *r*. That gave him *nevermore*. Then he had the problem of why in the world it should be repeated at the end of every stanza, because he thought in terms of ending every stanza with the same word. He said: Why should a reasonable being keep on saying *nevermore?* Then he thought of an unreasonable being—and at first he thought of a parrot. But of course a parrot is green and would do him no good. Then he thought of a raven. A raven's black. That's the right color. Then the black had to stand out, so he thought of marble, and that gave him the bust of Pallas, and so on. So through a link of reasoning he came to the poem "The Raven." He said the poem should not be too long since, if it is read at two sittings, then attention dissolves, and it cannot be followed. It cannot be too short either, because a short poem would not be intense. So he said to himself, I will write a poem of a hundred lines. In fact, he wrote a hundred and seven or ninety-seven, or whatever it may be. He also thought: What is the most tragic subject on earth? And he immediately answered: The most tragic subject on earth is the death of a beautiful woman. And who can lament her death best? Of course he thought her lover. That gave him the lover and the death of a perfect woman. But he thought that poetry could not happen in too wide a scope, so he needed a closed room. Then he thought of a library, and that of course would be the right place for the bust of Pallas. Then there should be a contrast. Since the raven had to enter into the poem, he would have to be driven in by the stormy night. Thus, by a link of reason, he went on to write down his poem. I suppose this is merely a hoax. Poe was very fond of hoaxes. I don't think anybody could write a poem in that way. But let us suppose that we accept the first of his arguments. Well, he might have argued: I need an unreasonable being, let's say, a madman. But no, he chose a bird, a raven. From my own poor experience, I know that poems do not get written in that way, and Poe wrote much that were poems according to that system. But I think of writing poetry and of reasoning as being essentially different. I should say there are two ways of thinking. One is the argument and the other is the myth. The Greeks could do both things at the same time. In, for example, that last conversation of Socrates before he drinks the hemlock, you find reason and myth wound together. But today it seems we have lost that capacity. We are either using arguments or we are using metaphors or images or fables. I suppose the real way of writing poetry is to let yourself be passive to dream. You do not try to reason it out. Of course you will reason out the details, the meter, the patterns of rhymes you will follow, the cadences, but as to the rest, it is given to you in the form of myths. Now all this comes out of our image of Edgar Allan Poe. And it is important that I should think of him as being unhappy. Unhappiness is part of that image, as much as unhappiness is part of the image of an old character, Hamlet. And were I to choose from the works of Poe, I suppose I would choose "The Narrative of Arthur Gordon Pym." But why choose? Why not have all the stories? Why not have, for example, "The Facts in the Case of M. Valdemar," "The Pit and the Pendulum," "The Gold Bug." All those stories are quite different from each other, and yet in all of them we hear the voice of Poe, and we are still hearing it at this moment.

BARNSTONE: One of Whitman's myths was that he was dealing with the common man and woman, that he was dealing with vernacular speech, with historical events such as the Civil War, with the death of Lincoln, which he celebrated in "When Lilacs Last in the Dooryard

Bloomed," another historical event. In your own writing, you have this aspect of dealing with the vernacular, with hooligans, with rough people, with death, ordinary life.

BORGES: Well, those are literary tricks.

BARNSTONE: Are not the literary tricks of the ordinary man, meaning what you have in common with Whitman, complemented by some other aspects of Poe, that is, the nightmare, the dream, the invention, the imagination, the erudition, sometimes sham, but there, sometimes the spoofing at erudition, the hoax, are you in part Poe and Whitman?

BORGES: I am indebted to both of them, as all contemporary poets are, and as all contemporary poets should be. As to nightmare and Poe, it's very strange. I have read many books of psychology, and little is said of the nightmare, and yet the nightmare stands apart. In Spanish the word for it is quite ugly, *pesadilla,* it can hardly be used. In Greek they have a fine word, *ephialtēs,* standing for the demon of the night. Now, I have a nightmare every other night. I am often haunted by nightmare. And I feel that were I a theologian—happily I am not—I might find an argument in favor of hell. It is very common to be unhappy, but when we are unhappy, we do not get the nightmare touch, the uncanny touch, the eerie touch. That is given us by the nightmare itself. The nightmare has a peculiar horror to it. The nightmare, that tiger of the dream. It has a peculiar horror that has nothing to do with things that happen to us in waking life. And that horror might be a foretaste of hell. I don't believe in hell, of course, but there is something very strange about the nightmare, and nobody seems to have noticed that. I have read many books on dreams—Havelock Ellis, for example. But I have never found any reference to that uncanny and very strange taste of the nightmare. Yet there it is, and it may be a gift, for all we know. I have been given plots for stories in nightmares, and I know them only too well, I have them very often and they always follow the same pattern. I have the nightmare of the labyrinth. I always begin by being at some particular place in Buenos Aires. Now that place may be a street corner I know well. It may be, for example, Venezuela or Perú or Arenaldes, Esmeralda. I know that is the place, but it is quite different. In nightmare what I see is actually marshes, mountains, hills, sometimes cattle and horses. But I know that I am on that particular street in Buenos Aires, which is quite unlike what I see, and I know that I have to find my way home and that

I won't. And then I know that this is the nightmare of the labyrinth. Because I keep on moving and coming back to the same place over and over again, to the same room over and over again. One of the nightmares. The other is the nightmare of the mirror. I see myself looking up, and then I see somebody I don't know, someone unknown to me, and I know that I am that being, and when that happens I awake and I am trembling all over. So my nightmares always follow the same pattern. But we seem to be straying farther from Poe.

BARNSTONE: I think we have strayed from Poe because you have strayed into that strange notion of reality, meaning dream and nightmare, which is so characteristic of your work and Poe's work.

BORGES: Poe's work of course and also of idealism. As to thinking of the world as unreal I am always thinking of it and am always surprised by the world, by the things that are happening to me. For example, last year I was eighty, and I thought nothing can happen to me. Then after that I underwent a successful but very painful operation. After that I went on a wonderful trip to Japan, a country I now greatly love and had not known before, and now strangely enough, here I am in Indiana, talking to you. All those things the future had in store for me, all those gifts, and I was quite unaware of it. And now it has come. And I keep on expecting more gifts from the future. Since the one thing we know about the future is that it will be quite unlike the present. People only think of the future in terms of the twentieth century magnified and distorted. But I know firstly that there will be many futures, and secondly that things that we think of as being important will be frivolous and irrelevant in the future. For example, men will not be politically minded, men will no longer be equal—it is an illusion—men will not think in terms of circumstances, of success, of failure. I expect a quite different world, and many different worlds. Not the brave new world of Huxley, which is merely a transformation of Hollywood. I know that many futures are about to come. Why speak of *the* future? That has no meaning.

BARNSTONE: I wonder whether we could finish our talk by your saying something about Robert Frost. Perhaps you remember by heart his poem "Acquainted with the Night"?

BORGES:

> I have been one acquainted with the night.
> I have walked out in rain—and back in rain.
> I have outwalked the furthest city light.

And at the end, we get the same line "I have been one acquainted with the night." In the beginning, at the first reading, you think that acquainted with the night means: I have walked through a city at night. But then you foresee, as you come to the last lines, that the night stands for evil, especially for sensual evil as felt by a Puritan, because

> One luminary clock against the sky
> Proclaimed the time was neither wrong nor right.
> I have been one acquainted with the night.

And that, I think, is the chief achievement of Frost. He could write poems that seem simple, but every time you read them you are delving deeper and finding many winding paths and many different senses. So Frost has given us a new idea of metaphor. He gives us metaphor in such a way that we take it as a simple, straightforward statement. And then you find that it is a metaphor. "And miles to go before I sleep/ And miles to go before I sleep." There we see that the same words have two different meanings. In the first of the last two verses, the words stand for miles and going and sleeping. And in the last line, sleep stands for death. But in a very unobtrusive way. He was a shy man, I suppose. But I think of him as being, perhaps, the greatest poet of the century, if "greatest poet" means anything. I think of Frost as being perhaps a finer poet than the other candidate, and that would be William Butler Yeats. I prefer Frost, but that would be a personal bias. Of course I revere Yeats. When I think back to such lines as "That dolphin-torn, that gong-tormented sea." That of course is gorgeous writing, the kind of writing that Frost tried to avoid, that I try to avoid also. But Yeats could also write straightforward verses. For example:

> How can I, that girl standing there,
> My attention fix
> On Roman or on Russian
> Or on Spanish politics?

Then:

> And maybe what they say is true
> Of war and war's alarms,
> but O that I were young again
> And held her in my arms!

AUDIENCE: I would like to know what you think of the Nobel Prize, and what Borges, the other Borges, thinks of it.

BORGES: I think that both of them feel very greedy about it. But they'll never get it.

BARNSTONE: The Nobel Prize committee keeps failing each year.

AUDIENCE: I'd like to hear you speak more about Old English, perhaps only because I love it also, Anglo-Saxon.

BORGES: I remember a disciple of mine, a fellow student, who said: "What a pity, what a pity, the battle of Hastings! Now Anglo-Saxon has come down to English, and we have to put up with Shakespeare. What a pity!" Really, I fell in love with Old English. I think that perhaps the Old English sounds, the open vowels, the hard Scottish *r*s, are better than the hushed English we speak today. It has a more resonant ring to it. That's the reason. My memory is full of Old English verses. In Old English poetry we are getting the impression that the poems have been composed, have been chanted by or, rather, given to the brave and simple man. They did not abound in vanity. Vanity might have been found in the kennings. But the Anglo-Saxons very soon found out that the kennings did them no good and so they became merely synonyms. They were the first to speak out. I remember the elegies, the beginning of *The Seafarer:* "I can now tell a true song about myself./ I can tell my travels," *Maeg ic be me sylfum soðgied wrecan,/ sipas secgan.** There the first lines are really Walt Whitman. In Old English poetry you get something essential, not only to England, but to all the world. You get the sea. The sea is always around the corner in Old English poetry. Even in that very dreary poem *Beowulf,* you find the sea in the beginning:

> Men ne cunnon
> secgan to soðe, selerædende,
> hæleð under heofenum, hwa þæm hlæste onfeng.†

There is the sea. And of course in *The Seafarer,* where he speaks of the bitterness and of the attraction of the sea. People have thought of *The Seafarer* as being a dialogue. That, I think, is wrong. We should think of it as being written by one man who had been defeated by the sea, who had suffered but went on loving it. Perhaps that piece is the best of all we have left of Anglo-Saxon literature. But there is also a poem written after the Battle of Hastings, and done into English by Longfellow. The

---

*Lines 1–2.
†*Beowulf,* lines 42, 50–52.

poem "The Grave." Longfellow translates: "Doorless is that house,/ And dark it is within."* But if you go back to the original you find still better: *Dureless is ðæt hus/ And deerc hit is wiðinnen.*

AUDIENCE: Could you elaborate more on your relationship with Ariosto, or your feelings about Italian literature and Dante?

BORGES: I think that the *Divine Comedy* is perhaps the peak of all literature. And I think I am in the right, because there is no other cause that would make me love that thing. For example, I have no Italian blood as far as I know. I am not a Catholic. I cannot accept the mythology of the poem. I cannot think of hell, of purgatory, and of heaven. And yet I know that Dante is right every time. In the case of Shakespeare, we are being let down at any moment. In the case of Dante, he is very dependable. He won't let you down. He knows what he's doing. There is another strange point I would like to tell you. It is Dante's idea that in a lifetime there is only a single moment. That moment stands for years and years of life, or stands for a man. For example, we are told nothing whatever of Paolo and Francesca. We know nothing about their political opinions, if any, of their ideas, if any, but we know that they were reading a book that came out of Britanny and that suddenly they knew that the characters in the book were themselves, and they knew that they were in love. That is sufficient. So Dante chooses a moment in every life. That is sufficient for him, since from that particular moment he gives us the whole character of the man and his whole life. That character may last three verses, and yet, there he is, forever. That is one of the feats of Dante. One of the many feats of Dante. As I have never studied Italian, I began by reading Longfellow's translation. And reading the notes. Then I had a bilingual edition, and I read, firstly, the English text, a canto, then the Italian text. I went on, and when I refound myself in purgatory, I could do without the English text and go on reading in Italian. To try to translate Dante into Spanish is a mistake, since the two languages are so much alike that anybody can understand them both. Besides, the Italians have made a very fine job of it. I have read the *Divine Comedy* through already some ten or twelve times. Every time in a different edition, and have been given new interpretations. Ariosto has also meant much to me. In fact, I wrote a poem called "Ariosto and the Arabs." Therein I

*Lines 24–25.

lamented that nobody seemed to read Ariosto since the *Arabian Nights* had taken over, and we don't even read the *Arabian Nights* as we should. But we have forgotten Ariosto and we should not forget him. Those two works, the *Furioso* and the *Arabian Nights,* resemble each other in the fact that they are really endless. And the fact that we are reading very long *is* a virtue. They have to be long. A labyrinth has to be long.

11

I Always Stood
in Fear of Mirrors

Indiana University,
April 1980

I always stood in fear of mirrors. When I was a little boy, there was something awful at my house. In my room we had three full-length mirrors. Then also the furniture was of mahogany, and that made a kind of dark mirror, like the mirror to be found in Saint Paul's epistle. I stood in fear of them, but being a child I did not dare say anything.

ALBERTO COFFA: All Borges readers are familiar with the fact that his favorite philosophers tend to be related to the idealist tradition, and Schopenhauer is certainly one of those.

JORGE LUIS BORGES: Hume, Berkeley, and Schopenhauer, yes.

COFFA: So perhaps starting with the easiest and silliest questions and then proceeding to still silly but nonetheless less silly questions—

BORGES: We will be as silly as we can!

COFFA: I might start with the following. Borges was quoted as saying about Schopenhauer: "Today, were I to choose a single philosopher, I would choose him. If the riddle of the universe can be stated in words, I think those words would be in his writings."

BORGES: Have I said that, really?

COFFA: I think you have. Did you agree with this?

BORGES: Of course I agree.

COFFA: In his biography of Borges, Rodríguez Monegal raises the question—

BORGES: I haven't read it. I have read no biography about myself.

COFFA: Well, you lived it, that's better.

BORGES: I underwent it, yes.

COFFA: He raises the question of what the nature of Schopenhauer's influence was, and he makes a conjecture, which I would like to read and ask you how you feel about it. Is he right or wrong or something in between? "In Schopenhauer, Borges may have found the notion that art is the only way to meaning. That art, as much as science, creates a meaningful natural cosmos out of the crumbling social order." So taking this quotation as an excuse, you might tell us whether this is close to the truth.

BORGES: I wonder whether the crumbling social order has anything to do with philosophy. I think philosophy is eternal. But as for the first part of the question you asked?

COFFA: The very beginning of his point is that in Schopenhauer, Borges may have found the notion that art is the only way to meaning.

BORGES: Well, I can hardly agree to that. I suppose *all* language is a way to meaning. Every single thing in the world may be used for meaning. But why art should be the only one, I am at a loss to understand.

COFFA: You have a poem to Sarmiento, who happens to be an Argentine political hero.

BORGES: He is the one man of genius we have produced, and perhaps the poet Almafuerte also. The others are men of talent only.

COFFA: In this poem, you contrast him—

BORGES: I wonder what I said about Sarmiento.

COFFA: Well, I'll tell you what you said about Sarmiento.

BORGES: Thank you, I am curious.

COFFA: You'll probably disagree, but you contrast him to what you call the white heroes of Argentine politics, those people—

BORGES: You mean the founding fathers, what we call the *próceres*.

COFFA: That's right, like maybe Washington here or Bolívar in Bolivia.

BORGES: Or maybe San Martín.

COFFA: People who are so ambiguous that anyone will admire them, regardless of politics. On the other hand, Sarmiento is hated by half the Argentines and loved by the other half, even today.

BORGES: Which is a proof that he is still living, that he still has enemies and friends.

COFFA: Now this brings me to Schopenhauer, in a mysterious way.

BORGES: Very mysterious to me.

COFFA: Here it comes. I wonder when we try to test Schopenhauer, using this criterion of his ability to be unequivocal, aren't you worried by the fact that Schopenhauer can be admired and taken as an example both by such a nice man as Mr. Borges and by such a nasty fellow as Otto Dietrich Tzurlinde, the concentration camp leader, in a story of yours, as a matter of fact.

BORGES: Yes, of course I remember. It comes back to me.

COFFA: Doesn't that bother you?

BORGES: No, I suppose that we are both in the right, if we admire Schopenhauer.

COFFA: But why does it bother you that San Martín and all the other white heroes can be all things to all people, and you prefer the unambiguous Schopenhauer, but it doesn't bother you that Schopenhauer can be taken by the Nazis to mean what they say and on the other hand he can be taken by you to mean what you want to say.

BORGES: Schopenhauer can be used by the Nazis, but that means they haven't understood him. Even as Nietzsche. Nietzsche, for example, said, when the German empire was founded: "Another empire, another tomfoolery." But he has been used by the Nazis. Yet Schopenhauer was his master, and certainly they were anything but nationalists. I hate all nationalism. I try to be a cosmopolitan, to be a citizen of the world. And also I am a good Argentine citizen. The Argentine Republic is part of the world.

COFFA: Some people would challenge that.

BORGES: What *is* it a part of? Of hell, of purgatory?

COFFA: Probably.

BORGES: Paradise?

COFFA: No, not paradise.

BORGES: No, not paradise, certainly not. That may be unattainable, or nonexistent. While hell is with us all the time, or most of the time. Not today of course.

COFFA: What is, then, the right interpretation of Schopenhauer? What is it in Schopenhauer that attracted you so very early on?

BORGES: Schopenhauer, if I remember rightly, wrote that he had but one idea: *Die Welt als Wille und Vorstellung* "the world as will and idea," and that the shortest way to explain that idea might be found in the two very pleasant volumes he wrote. That, he said, is the shortest way. I know no other. But what I am really saying all the time is *Die Welt als Wille und Vorstellung.* Of course I have to clarify it, since those words in themselves are more or less meaningless. And of course what Schopenhauer called *Wille* is the same thing as Bergson's *élan vital* and Bernard

Shaw's "life force." They amount to the same thing. And as for *Vorstellung,* I suppose it is the same idea that you get in Buddhism, the idea of *maya,* of illusion, of things not existing in themselves but only as phenomena. In the case of Schopenhauer, I think I have also been reading him throughout my life because he is a charming writer. Philosophers are not expected to be charming. And yet philosophers wrote quite well before Kant and Hegel. Then they evolved a peculiar jargon of their own. While in the past Plato was a fine writer, Saint Augustine was a fine writer, Descartes was a fine writer. And then of course we have Locke, Hume, and Berkeley, they were fine writers also, and so was Schopenhauer. But today philosophy seems to be linked to some kind of uncouth jargon.

COFFA: Rodríguez Monegal says that you used to meet with your father and Macedonio Fernández to talk about philosophy and that you did talk about Schopenhauer. What were the things that you discussed?

BORGES: I remember when I was a boy my father taught me the essential riddles, the essential problems, of philosophy without using any proper name or any date. For example, he would take the chessboard, and using the chessboard as a tool, he would give me the paradoxes of Zeno, of the Presocratics, and not speaking about them. Or I remember a night when we were at home, he asked me—he held an orange in his hand, we were having dinner—and he asked me: "What color is this orange?" Then I said: "Well, I suppose it's orange color." But I found out that was not sufficient and said: "Let's say between red and yellow." And he said: "Yes, but if I put out the light or if you close your eyes. . . . " Then I stared at him. The next night he would ask me: "What's the taste of the orange?" And I said: "Well, orange taste." And he would say: "Do you really think that the orange is tasting its own flavor all day long and all night long?" And I said: "Well, I won't go as far as that." And then he would ask me: "What's the weight of this orange?" And then he held it in his hand. And so I slid on to idealism, without the word idealism being used. But I was being led, not to understanding, but to sensing, a feeling for the paradoxes of Zeno, and yet he had never mentioned those things. Afterwards, he gave me a book, a book by Lewis, a Jew, a friend of George Eliot, and the book was called *A Biographical History of Philosophy.* I still have that book by me at home. And therein I found that all those jokes, all those puzzlements of my father, all were to be found in that book and were called idealism, Presocratic philosophy, and so on. I was led to them by my father, who knew how to teach. He was a professor of psychology; he thoroughly disbelieved in psychology. But he taught me in that very pleasant way, by asking plain questions. He taught me philosophy by means of the orange and the chessboard. Then I have gone in for feeling those problems myself. Sometimes I lie awake and I ask myself, Who am I? or even What am I? What am I doing? And I think of time flowing on. I remember a very fine line that Tennyson wrote when he was fifteen: "Time flowing through the middle of the night." Of course that's Newton's time, I suppose. *Tempus absoluto.* And there are other lines about time, since time is such a fine subject. It seems to be the *one* subject to me. It seems to me to be the *essential* riddle. If we knew what time is—though of course we never shall—then we would know who we are and what we are. Since the problem of identity is like the problem of time. The fact that I am here with you today and that I'll be in Buenos Aires within ten days, and that I remember periods in Uruguay and in the Argentine when I was a boy. And all those things belong to me in a fashion that I cannot express, that I cannot understand. But I will go on trying to solve these problems, knowing of course that all my attempts will be useless, and that the pleasure lies not in the answer but in the riddle.

COFFA: In connection with your interest in idealism, you encountered solipsism, in fact you refered to solipsism last time in your talk about poetry.

BORGES: The central idea of solipsism is that there's only one individual. I am an individual, but also every single one of you is an individual. And all the rest has been dreamed by him. For example, let's say, the sky, the stars, the round earth, and all history, all that is a dream. Of course if you are going to accept solipsism as absolute, then the world begins when I rap the table thus. No, it didn't begin then, because that is already past. That already happened very, very long ago within a snap, the second I tapped on the table. You go on and on, and you never finish of course. I suppose if we were really solipsists, we would think of the present as existing, and not of the past and the future. But since the present glides on, we have to accept a tiny amount of past and a tiny amount of future. Those should be accepted. Then that leads us, alas, to universal history, to the whole past of the world, to the future, and so on.

COFFA: When I was preparing for this conversation, I thought I had to explain to the audience what solipsism is before I asked my questions about it, but I found a very serious problem.

BORGES: Now, solipsism, I think, was discovered by Descartes, who rejected it. Nobody seems to have accepted solipsism. At least I have read Bradley's and Bertrand Russell's refutation of solipsism. I have never read anything in proof of it, or accepting it. I have only read refutations.

COFFA: Yes, and mostly by people who say that it is irrefutable.

BORGES: Yes, irrefutable at the same time that they can hardly be convinced. That's what Hume said about Berkeley, no? "His arguments are incapable of refutation and produce no conviction." Those are David Hume's words.

COFFA: Which is true of most philosophical arguments.

BORGES: I suppose, yes. But I remember that Emerson wrote: Arguments convince nobody. And Walt Whitman also felt that arguments were no good. But we might be convinced by the night air, by the wind, by looking at the stars, but not by arguments.

COFFA: We will return to idealism in a moment, but I would like to ask you a question concerning a philosopher who did not influence you significantly, as far as I can tell, the Spanish philosopher Ortega. I don't mean to ask a question about him but rather a discussion that you had—

BORGES: Did I?

COFFA: You did, yes. On a subject which he wrote about, which is not surprising since he wrote about every subject, I am told.

BORGES: I haven't read him.

COFFA: The discussion had to do with Ortega's theory of the novel. Roughly speaking, what he was saying is that—

BORGES: That it is impossible to invent a new plot. People are inventing new plots all the time. For example, detective story writers are inventing new plots all the time.

COFFA: That's right, he was appealing to the distinction between substance and function, and he argued that whereas until 1900, not only science, but also literature had been based on the idea of function and no serious attention had been paid to the substance—

BORGES: Substance and function, what do you mean exactly? I can hardly follow you.

COFFA: I'm quoting him.

BORGES: But he has to be paraphrased in order to be understood. What did he mean by function? Did he mean the plot?

COFFA: I would suppose that he meant the structure of the novel quite independently of the psychology of the characters.

BORGES: It depends. In the case of a short tale, the plot is all-important. But in the case of a novel, then the plot may be thought away. What is really important is the characters. Or maybe in a short story by Henry James, both are important. Or in a short story by Kipling, both are important—the plot and what is called very loosely the psychology of the characters. But to take a famous example, *Don Quixote,* even in the case of that famous novel, one thinks of the adventures as being little more than adjectives of the character. They are attributes of him. We need them in order to know *him.* All the adventures of Don Quixote are adjectives of Don Quixote. They are all meant to show us the kind of man he was. In a hidden sense of course. The adventures taken by themselves are irrelevant and rather poor. But they serve a function, because after reading *Don Quixote* we know who he was. We have been Don Quixote or Alonso Quijano all the time when we are reading the book. And that might be said of many novels, for example, the novels of George Meredith, *The Egoist,* and so on. Those are meant to show character. While in other novels, what is important is the action and the surprise you get at the end. In most novels of adventure, I should say in Stevenson's *Treasure Island* and in the *Arabian Nights,* what is important is the adventures and not the characters. The characters could hardly exist without the adventures. The adventures are all-important.

COFFA: It would seem that what Ortega was arguing for was—

BORGES: I suppose that Ortega had read very few novels, no?

COFFA: I wouldn't know.

BORGES: Well, he had no English, so he missed the best novels in the world.

COFFA: I don't know about that. But it seems to be that he was arguing that we have run out of plots . . .

BORGES: I don't think we have. I seem to be inventing new plots all the time. I don't seem to have run dry of plots.

COFFA: I think you are right. But in any case, he seemed to be saying—

BORGES: I know. What he wanted was novels like *Marius the Epicurean* by Pater, no? Novels in which practically nothing happens, which are made for an old man. I suppose he was after that kind of novel, no?

COFFA: Proust, although Proust was perhaps a bit too much even for him.

BORGES: Yes, Henry James, Meredith, Pater.

COFFA: What you call the psychological novel.

BORGES: I personally can enjoy both kinds of novel. I enjoy plots and I enjoy characters.

COFFA: Since he enjoyed it, being a philosopher, he thought he had to prove that that was the only admissible sort of thing.

BORGES: Let me think, in the case of Shakespeare, you believe in the characters, you don't believe in the plots. We all believe in Hamlet. He is far more real than I am. But I don't believe in his father's ghost, in the mother of his father. I can't bring myself to believe in the plot. In the case of Macbeth also. I believe in Macbeth, in Lady Macbeth. Even in the three witches who are also fates, but I can't believe the plot.

COFFA: So there is the psychological novel, on the one hand, where the all-important thing is the characters, and what happens to them is not so important—

BORGES: In the case of Conrad, I suppose *both* are important. I think of Conrad as being a chief novelist. In the case of Conrad, what do you make of him? One thinks of him in terms of the story and of the characters. So really there is no opposition. We have now said both things.

COFFA: But in your own writings, or at least in many of them, the plot is what attracts attention much more than the characters.

BORGES: The fact is that I cannot create characters. I am always writing about myself in impossible situations. I have never created a single character, as far as I know. In my stories I suppose the only character is myself, and I disguise myself as a gaucho, as a *compadrito,* * and so on, but it is myself all the time, really. Myself in imaginary times or in imaginary situations. I haven't created characters.

COFFA: Except for yourself.

BORGES: Yes. But if we think of Dickens, we are thinking in terms of multitudes. In the case of Shakespeare also. In the case of Balzac, I am told the same thing happens, but I haven't actually read him.

COFFA: Here comes my question.

BORGES: At long last. Sorry.

COFFA: They haven't come to hear my questions.

BORGES: I have come to hear your questions.

COFFA: The psychological novel, Ortega says, is the only good thing to do, and there are lots of people doing it nowadays. Then there is this other kind of writing.

* "Street hoodlum," translated elsewhere as "streetcorner man."

BORGES: Contrivance.

COFFA: Which you claim is very much alive and well, which you practice, together with Adolpho Bioy Casares and several other people, and which seems to have been influential in South America. I won't say Latin America because otherwise you'll tell me that there is no such thing.

BORGES: Yes. The whole thing's a fiction, yes.

COFFA: The question is: Have they had anything to do with your decision not to write psychological novels and to write these other sorts of things? And before you answer me, I'd like to read a passage from something you wrote.

BORGES: Yes, but I would like to say that I don't write what I want. Those things are given me by something or somebody. You can call it the muse or the Holy Ghost or the subconscious. I don't choose my subjects or plots. They are given to me. I have to stand back and receive them in a passive moment.

COFFA: Do we have a copy of *Other Inquisitions?*

BORGES: If not, you can invent anything you like.

COFFA: I would like you to comment on something that you say in "For Bernard Shaw," from *Other Inquisitions.*

BORGES: Oh, did I?

COFFA: You did.

BORGES: I wrote those things a long time ago and I'm an old gentleman now, over eighty. I cannot be expected to remember what I wrote. I never reread my own writing. I try to remember other and better authors.

COFFA: "The character of man and his variations is the essential theme of the contemporary novel. Lyric poetry is the complacent magnification of happiness and unhappiness."

BORGES: Did I write that?

COFFA: Yes, you did.

BORGES: It's quite good, eh?

COFFA: "The philosophies of Heidegger and Jaspers—"

BORGES: Have I written that?

COFFA: Yes. But let me finish the sentence.

BORGES: I've never read them.

COFFA: "—transform every one of us into an interesting interlocutor of a secret and continuous dialogue with nothingness or God." So we have lyric poetry on the one hand, existentialist philosophies on the other.

BORGES: I have only read Alexius Meinong's existentialist philosophy.

COFFA: "These disciplines that formally may be admirable encourage that illusion of the I or ego that the Vedanta disapproves of as a capital error."

BORGES: It is also condemned by the Buddha, I think, no? By Hume.

COFFA: And by Schopenhauer.

BORGES: By Schopenhauer and by my friend Macedonio Fernández.

COFFA: "They play at desperation and anguish, but in the end they flatter our vanity. In that sense they are immoral." So we have lyric poetry, Heidegger's and Jasper's works being in the end immoral, and then we have the work of Shaw, which you offer as a paradigm of the opposite approach and which "leaves an aftertaste of liberation."

BORGES: I suppose someone worked in the names of Heidegger and Jaspers.

COFFA: Could you comment?

BORGES: Yes. Of course I can. At least I'll do my best. I think that the novel is really flattering the reader because the reader becomes an interesting character, while in the epic, for example, the reader is not made to analyze his unhappiness. And in that sense you might think of the novel as being immoral. But you might also think of Hamlet, Prince of Denmark, as being immoral. Or of Beider, since he encourages introspection, abounding, as Kipling had it, in loud self-pity, which is encountered by the novel, but which is *not* encouraged by the epic, or by writers with an epic strain to them, for example, Joseph Conrad or George Bernard Shaw.

COFFA: The farfetched conjecture that I wanted you to refute was the following: that you are not very much interested in the psychological novel because you don't find that there is anything to the ego, and at any rate that there is anything interesting in the ego.

BORGES: I think that the psychological novel makes for any amount of make-believe and lying. You can say anything in a psychological novel. So and so was so happy that he committed suicide. That may be in a novel, but not in a tale, I should say. In the novel, anything is possible. The idea of loving and hating people at the same time. Well, psychoanalysis is a kind of novel. Or gossip.

COFFA: So would you say, or is this thoroughly wrongheaded, that the psychological novel is based on a wrong philosophy, on a philosophy that like Heidegger's and Jasper's philosophy and lyrical poetry has even something ethically wrong about it.

BORGES: Yes, I would venture to say so, at least today, and now. I wonder how I will feel about it tomorrow, or the day after tomorrow. But today, yes, I thoroughly agree. There is something wrong about the psychological novel. And about the romantic movement, sentimentalism. Those kinds of things should be subdued rather than encouraged.

COFFA: Would it be fair to relate the psychological novel to a realist attitude?

BORGES: I suppose it would.

COFFA: And your magical and fantastic literature to an idealistic way of looking at things—idealism at least concerning the conception of the ego?

BORGES: I tend to think of things as being illusory. The idea of the world as a dream is not alien to me. On the contrary. But I know that when I write I have to enrich the dream, I have to add something to the dream. Let's say, I have to add patterns to the dream. As to realism, I always thought it was essentially false. I have no use, let's say, for local color, for being true to history. Those things are alien to me. What I like—there is a fine word in English—is to dream away, to let myself go dreaming. That's what I really enjoy. But afterwards, of course I have to go to the task of writing it down, of correcting the proofs, of emending the sentences. But really, I think of a writer as a man who is continually dreaming. I am continually dreaming, and I may be dreaming you at the present moment for all I know. Solipsism again.

COFFA: You have said that universal history is the history of a few metaphors.

BORGES: I suppose I was making a fine sentence when I wrote that. I wonder if it is really true, eh? It might be said, and it has a fine ring to it. That should be enough, no? "Universal history is the history of a few metaphors." Yes. I was taken in when I wrote that. I'm taken in now. Maybe you're taken in. I am *not* at the present moment. Universal history is far more. History is what James Joyce called it: a nightmare, from which we are all trying to awaken.

COFFA: A closely related claim that you make and that you are perhaps more committed to than the one I just read is that literature is the exploration of the finite and a rather small number of metaphors.

BORGES: It is true. I think that there are but few metaphors. I think that the idea of inventing new metaphors may be wrong. We have, for example, time and the river, living and dreaming, sleeping and dying, the eyes and the stars. Those should be sufficient. And yet, some ten days ago I read a metaphor that greatly surprised me. It came from an Indian poet: "And therein I found the Himalayas are the laughter of Shiva." That is to say, a terrible god for a terrible mountain. Now that metaphor is new, at least it is new to me; I can't link it to stock metaphors I have used. The idea of the mountains as being the laughter of Shiva. I thought I had found new metaphors in Chesterton, and then I found that they were not really new. For example, when a Danish Viking is made to say, in *The Ballad of the White Horse:* "And Marble like solid moonlight,/ And gold like a frozen fire."* Those metaphors are of course impossible. And yet the idea of comparing white marble and a white moon, or fire and gold, is not new. But they are expressed in a new way. When Chesterton writes

> But I shall not grow too old to see
> Enormous night arise,
> A cloud that is larger than the world
> And a monster made of eyes†

we might think of this as being new. But of course the idea of eyes and stars have always gone together. So what Chesterton has done is to give a new shape to those very ancient and, I should say, essential metaphors.

COFFA: You yourself use a small number of metaphors.

BORGES: I remember what Emerson said: language is fossil poetry. He said every word is a metaphor. You can verify that by looking a word up in the dictionary. All words are metaphors—or fossil poetry, a fine metaphor itself.

COFFA: You have the mirrors image, you have the dreams, you have a bag of tricks as some people have called it.

BORGES: Yes, I have a few stock subjects. A bag of tricks, yes. But those things are given to me. I cannot elude them. I cannot write without those tricks.

COFFA: I am not blaming you for using them.

BORGES: Those tricks are essential to me. They are not arbitrary. I have not chosen them, they have chosen me.

COFFA: They have good taste. Mirrors, for example?

BORGES: I always stood in fear of mirrors. When I was a little boy,

*Book III, stanza 21, lines 110–11.
†"A Second Childhood," lines 27–30.

there was something awful at my house. In my room we had three full-length mirrors. Then also the furniture was of mahogany, and that made a kind of dark mirror, like the mirror to be found in Saint Paul's epistle. I stood in fear of them, but being a child I did not dare say anything. So every night I was confronted by three or four images of myself. I felt that to be really awful. I never said anything, since childhood is shy.

COFFA: It seems to me that most of these metaphors that I have seen in your writings are in some sense used to support some version of idealism, if I may use that argument.

BORGES: I suppose they do. My idea of the "fetch," the *Doppelgänger* in German, the double in Jekyll and Hyde.

COFFA: Which we find in "Tlön" where you have the heresiarch say that mirrors and copulation are hateful because they multiply the images of man.

BORGES: I think the images of mankind and the images in the mirror are equally unreal and equally real. Mirrors and copulation are the same thing. They stand for creating images, not realities.

COFFA: Similarly dreams, which are often put together with the other metaphors of circular regress or a regress—

BORGES: In time.

COFFA: Yes, ad infinitum, where dreamers—

BORGES: That Saint Augustine called "the circular labyrinth of the Stoics." They have history repeating itself all the time. I remember that very fine poem by Dante Gabriel Rossetti, based on the same idea:

> I have been here before,
>   But when or how I cannot tell:
> I know the grass beyond the door,
>   The sweet keen smell,
> The sighing sound, the lights around the shore.
>
> You have been mine before. . . .

The poem consists of three stanzas and is called "Sudden Light." When you suddenly feel that all this has already happened. What the French call *déjà vu*.

COFFA: Is it the case that through the use of these metaphors you are often trying to destroy the commonsense belief in the nature of the world that surrounds us?

BORGES: Progress.

COFFA: No. I didn't mean to ask about progress. Are you trying to create the impression that the world is not this solid—

BORGES: But really, I can bring myself to disbelieve in space. You might imagine a spaceless world, a world of music, for example. A world made entirely of sounds, of words, and of what they stood for. But I cannot imagine a timeless world. And yet, twice in my life I have had the experience of being in a timeless world. That was given me only twice throughout my life. I had been very unhappy one day—I felt suddenly that I was outside time. I don't know how long that lasted. It was a very strange experience.

COFFA: In your stories there are persons who manage to solve the riddle of the universe. As you say, if anyone has written on paper the answer to the riddle, Schopenhauer has. In your stories there are some people who succeed.

BORGES: They succeed, but I don't! They succeed as fancy characters. But I have no solution to propose.

COFFA: I'm not going to ask you. I only wanted you to comment on something funny that happens to these people when they solve the riddle of the universe.

BORGES: Of course they can't express it because I can't express it for them. They find out the answer but I don't know it, so I've got to concoct something to account for their silence.

COFFA: You've given the answer but I'm going to ask the question anyhow. It seems to me that the two opposite cases of the same situation are Carlos Daneri in the "Aleph" who, by observing the aleph, finally manages to observe the sun. Then he tries to say what he saw and writes a very nonsensical poem.

BORGES: Very nonsensical. Like most poets.

COFFA: On the other hand, there is Tzinacán, the magus of the pyramid of Qaholom, who also in some sense solved the riddle of the universe, but he decides not to talk . . .

BORGES: The reason is that I can't talk, since I don't know it.

COFFA: Is that really all that it is? Is it a trick?

BORGES: I'm afraid it's a trick. What can I do about it? I wrote that story oh so long ago.

COFFA: Shall I read the last paragraph? You'll like it.

Borges: Thank you. Yes, I hope I do. I wrote in a very baroque style in those days. It's a story about a leopard, no?*

Coffa: Yes. There is a leopard in it. It is the story about this priest or magus of the pyramid of Qaholom.

Borges: Then in the end he feels the power of god, of one of his gods.

Coffa: He deciphers the script of the leopard.

Borges: He's an Aztec I think, as far as I remember.

Coffa: Yes, that's right.

Borges: He had to be an Aztec because I needed a jaguar.

Coffa: "Let the mystery written on the tigers die with me."

Borges: Yes, because I think of the skin of a leopard as being writing.

Coffa: "He who has glimpsed the universe, he who has glimpsed the burning intentions of the universe cannot think of one man, of one man's trivial happiness or sorrows," even though that man be himself.

Borges: He is thinking of evil.

Coffa: "That man *has been he,* but now it does not matter to him."

Borges: Because now he is transfigured and the revelation is in somebody else. He no longer cares for the particular individual he was before he got there.

Coffa: There are these two people who uncover the riddle of the universe. One of them tries to talk and says the most idiotic things one could think of.

Borges: The other one chose silence because I can't find any words for him.

Coffa: Not only that but he adopts a Schopenhauerean view of the world.

Borges: I suppose that to him the word is *ineffable,* it's unspeakable, no? And he is right, because all words need something shared. If I use the word *yellow,* and if you have never seen yellow, you can't understand me. And if I know the absolute, and you haven't, you can't understand me. That's the real reason. All words imply a reality or an unreality shared by the speaker and by the hearer or by the reader and by the writer. But in many cases, in the case of ecstasies, that can only be told through metaphors, it cannot be told directly. It has to be told through metaphors. That is the reason why the mystics always resort to the same metaphors. A metaphor may be conceptual or a mystic might

*In the story it is a tiger.

talk in terms of the grape or the rose or of fleshly love also. Even the Persian mystics do, the Sufis.

COFFA: There is a philosopher who is very influential and who has been strongly influenced by the people you like most, Schopenhauer and Maltner, a philosopher you very much love. I mean Wittgenstein—

BORGES: Wittgenstein, of course, yes.

COFFA: — who claimed that the most important philosophical distinction to draw is a distinction between what can be said, which coincides with what can be thought, on the one hand, and what one might hope can be said, which philosophers are trying to say in their professional confusion, throughout their lives, but which can only be shown. The distinction is between saying and showing.

BORGES: I think of art as being an allusion. I think that you can only allude to things, you can never express them. This is of course against Bendetto Croce's theory. I can only allude to things. I may mention the moon but I cannot define the moon. But I may mention it, and that's allowed me, if I do it in an unobtrusive way.

COFFA: Perhaps your Tzinacán hero was of the same persuasion.

BORGES: I know very little about him.

COFFA: About as much as anyone else. But I would like to read you the last paragraph of a short story of yours, "The Wall and the Books."

BORGES: It's an essay really, not a story. But in a sense a story also.

COFFA: I have been told that you have blurred the distinction between the essay and the story, that thanks to you we no longer know where one stops and the other begins.

BORGES: And between verse and prose. I keep swaying to and fro.

COFFA: So I'll read the last paragraph.

BORGES: I'm all agog.

COFFA: "The tenacious wall, which at this moment, and at all moments, casts its system of shadows over lands I shall never see—"

BORGES: "System" is a good word because you have something regular and at the same time unknown. "System of shadows."

COFFA: "—is the shadow of a Caesar who ordered the most reverent of nations to burn its past."

BORGES: He was the first emperor, Shih Huang Ti, the Chinese emperor.

COFFA: It is plausible that this idea moves us in itself, aside from the conjectures it allows. Generalizing from the preceding case, we could infer that *all* forms have their virtue in themselves and not in any conjectural "content." This would concord with the thesis of Bendetto Croce. Already Pater in 1877 had affirmed that all arts aspire to the condition of music, which is pure form. "Music, states of happiness, mythology, faces belabored by time, certain twilights, and certain places try to tell us something, or have said something we should not have missed, or are about to say something; this imminence of a revelation which does not occur is, perhaps, the aesthetic phenomenon." I wonder if you have anything to add to this.

BORGES: I can only say that I agree, although I wrote it ever so many years ago. I have that feeling every now and then. But I get it especially when I look on the sea or on a plain or mountains, perhaps, or when I hear music. I feel I am about to receive something but I cannot express it. Yes, I have that feeling.

AFTERWORD

In Buenos Aires the silver glint of the street tiles defies the monotony of progress. Walls left pockmarked from old injuries of pastel patch and paint suffer at the hands of a people who, rather than cover such wounds, prefer to ponder them. A florist on a street corner, forgetting to sell a flower, discusses Kierkegaard. I stop at a newsstand and the vendor hands me the latest issue of *Gráfico,* the sports magazine. He turns the pages for me, stops at the description of last week's boxing feature at Luna Park, and begins to read. Suddenly, he looks up at me and announces gravely: "You see, Magarena lost again. So much technique and so little heart! No essence!"

I carry the magazine under my arm into the neighborhood where the blind man lives. It is a strange neighborhood. One day it is bright, colorful, alive. The next day it is gray, depressed, as if it is trying hard to die, to belong to some other place and time. I am reminded that *porteños,* the people of Buenos Aires, have no place, no time, either real or experiential. They move from one minute to another without ever resolving one moment. Life and death blend. As Borges has said, there is no past, only memory. There is no present, only a sense of consciousness. The future is never talked about.

Buenos Aires is a city of dreams and contemplation. Between 1890 and 1920 millions came to its port, not to live there, but to create their own realities while waiting for a ship to take them back. The boat never came. So they built the city like Rome and like Paris and like Seville. Since it was based on dreams it had to be perfect: slums had to be the most despairing; palaces, the most opulent; the stench of slaughterhouses on the Riachuelo, the most offensive. When the construction stopped, before the city could be defined, the pretense had to go on. The city was divided into more dreams. The English section of the north required one to speak English and discuss the merits of Old English literature. The Italian neighborhoods had to be louder and more grotesque than Naples. It is not a city to live in, it is a city to dream in, to escape. Its identity is pretense. Identities can be manipulated, can be touched. Dreams must confuse every possible reality.

I believe that Borges deeply loves Buenos Aires, its streets and its patios. But, like the city, he avoids identity. Once, driving late at night through the countryside of southern Indiana, Borges leaned over and said: "You know, Oclander, every dream I have is about Buenos Aires. Even if I know the dream is about London, it takes place on a street corner of Buenos Aires." Despite his denials the city exists within Borges as it exists within every *porteño.* When asked about his memories of early Buenos Aires, he answers:

171

"Really I saw very little of it . . . it never interested me . . . my memories are memories of the books I read." Still, his first question for a fellow Argentine is "What barrio are you from?" He recalls every house, every detail. Why the tension?

It is, in fact, the same tension that exists between the reality of death and Borges' dream of death in many of his short stories and poems. Why does Borges, the man of letters, the tranquil poet, glorify the violence of death in his writings? It is the value of the method, the suddenness, of death that defines life. Dying quietly, passing on, is unacceptable; if life is a creation, death too must be created. "El Sur," one of Borges' early stories, tells of a man dying in a hospital as he dreams of a fight in which he must die at the point of a knife. He thus "chooses" the form of his death because he cannot merely accept it. So, too, Borges cannot "pass on"; he must "dream on."

It strikes me as I walk through the streets near his home that, like his city, Borges indeed seeks no definition beyond what he creates: Rome or Paris, Iceland or Sarmiento's desert, the aristocrat or the savage gaucho. His journey from secret island to secret island is the legacy of Buenos Aires, both its beauty and its brutality. If a Borges poem is a beginning and an end dreamed, the rest to be created as a series of labyrinths that may or may not link the beginning and the end, so too is the city. Borges and Buenos Aires belong to the same dream.

The florist is no longer at the street corner and the news vendor is by now off to some café. Only the pockmarked walls and the street tiles glistening like haunting tears remain of the most secret of Borges' islands—Buenos Aires.

JORGE ISAIAS OCLANDER

JORGE LUIS BORGES
Biographical Note

Jorge Luis Borges was born in Buenos Aires in 1899. He was educated in Argentina and later in Switzerland and France. A major writer of our century, he has published many collections of short stories, essays, and poems, which have been translated into the world's principal languages. Often his stories read like erudite essays, his essays like poems, and his poems like brief narrations. Contending that the distinction between poetry and prose is largely typographical, he has included sections of prose in recent volumes of poetry. Throughout his work, Borges explores real, mythical, and metaphysical worlds, seeking absolute truths, key words, and escape from the labyrinth of solitude and confusion. At the same time he knows that his search, which justifies "the algebra of his being," will fail, for in our condition of Heraclitian flux there is no single truth, word, or escape from self.

Borges began to lose his sight in 1955, the year he started to study Anglo-Saxon and Old Norse, whose themes have profoundly influenced his work, especially his poetry. The poems reveal the ontological exploration, enormous erudition, and spoofing humor of his best *ficciones,* yet they also contain a personal pathos and self-delineation absent from his other writing. Borges has received many international honors, including the International Publishers' Prize in 1961, which he shared with Samuel Beckett, the Jerusalem Prize in 1971, and, in 1980, the Cervantes Prize, which was awarded him by the King of Spain. He was also knighted by the Queen of England, thus making him a companion of his closest friend and most esteemed knight, Alonso Quijano. He has received many honorary degrees, including the degree of Doctor of Letters, *honoris causa,* from Columbia, Oxford, and the University of Paris.

ABOUT THE PARTICIPANTS

JAIME ALAZRAKI, Professor of Spanish, Harvard University, is the author of numerous books of criticism, including *The Narrative Prose of Jorge Luis Borges* and *Versions, Inversions, Reversions: The Mirror as a Structural Model in the Stories of Borges.*

LUIS BELTRÁN, Professor of Spanish and Comparative Literature, Indiana University, has written several volumes of poetry, the novel *The Fruit of Her Womb,* and critical books on Federico García Lorca and Juan Ruiz' *The Book of Good Love.*

KENNETH BRECHER, Professor of Physics, Boston University, shares with Borges an interest in paradoxes and time. His published works in astrophysics include the book *Astronomy and the Ancients.*

DICK CAVETT, comedy writer, actor, and television personality, is the host of the interview program "The Dick Cavett Show," aired on PBS.

ALBERTO COFFA, Professor of the History and Philosophy of Science, Indiana University, is the author of numerous articles, including a philosophical study of Borges' use of time.

JOHN COLEMAN is Chairman of the Department of Spanish, New York University, and the author of *Notes on Borges and American Literature* and other books.

ROGER CUNNINGHAM received the Ph.D. degree in comparative literature from Indiana University in 1978.

ROBERT DUNN was Assistant Professor of English at Indiana University at the time of Borges' 1976 visit to Indiana.

MIGUEL ENGUÍDANOS, Professor of Spanish, Indiana University, edited *Jorge Luis Borges: His Best Pages.*

JORGE ISAIAS OCLANDER is Director of the Office of Latino Affairs, Indiana University.

175

ALASTAIR REID, distinguished essayist, poet, and Contributing Editor of the *New Yorker,* has translated many Spanish works, including Borges' *Gold of the Tigers.*

MARGERY RESNICK is Chairwoman of Foreign Languages and Literature, Massachusetts Institute of Technology, and author of *The Broken Rhythm: The Poems of Pedro Garfias* and several articles. She is the editor of *A World Bibliography of Translated Works of Women Writers.*

The Editor

WILLIS BARNSTONE, Professor of Comparative Literature and Latin American Studies, Indiana University, is an award-winning poet and the translator of works in Spanish (including the poems of Borges) and Ancient Greek. He has edited several poetry anthologies, including *Modern European Poetry, Greek Lyric Poetry,* and (with Aliki Barnstone) *A Book of Women Poets from Antiquity to Now.* His most recent volume is *The Poetics of Ecstasy.* Mr. Barnstone's book of photographs and poems, *New Faces of China,* was published by the Indiana University Press in 1973.